INTERROGATING THE CANON

INTERROGATING THE CANON
Literature and Pedagogy of Dalits

K. Purushotham

KALPAZ

ISBN: 978-93-5128-164-1
Price : ₹ 825/-

First Published, 2015

Published by

Kalpaz Publications
C-30, Satyawati Nagar,
Delhi-110052
Ph. : 9212142040
E-mail: kalpaz@hotmail.com

Printed at : G. Print Process, Delhi

Cataloging in Publication Data—DK

Courtesy: D.K. Agencies (P) Ltd. <docinfo@dkagencies.com>

Purushotham, K., author.

Interrogating the canon : literature and pedagogy of dalits / K. Purushotham.

pages cm

Includes bibliographical references (pages).

ISBN 9789351281641

1. Dalits in literature. 2. Telugu literature—Dalit authors—History and criticism. 3. Dalits—Education—India. I. Title.

DDC 894.82709 23

Contents

Acknowledgements

I would like to express my gratitude to all those who have been instrumental in shaping my thoughts, especially Prof A. Jaganmohana Chary, Prof Kancha Ilaiah, Prof Thirupathi Kumar, Gita Ramaswamy, N. Dharmapal and late Dr Kesaraj Kumar. I must also thank my colleagues and scholars for providing support, discussing with me and offering comments. My special thanks to J.L. Mandal for meticulously proofreading the draft. Above all I want to thank my wife, Madhuri, daughter, Spandana and son, Ashish for allowing me the academic space in spite of all the time it took me away from them. I would like to thank Kalpaz Publications, Delhi for bringing out this book so impressively and timely with a professional touch. I beg forgiveness of all those who have been with me in my academic endeavor, and whose help I might have failed to acknowledge. Thank you all.

Preface

The mainstream literary theory and criticism, being generic, is a form of subsumption of the specificities. In this respect, it is similar to India's mainstream nationalism that ignored the cultures of the marginals. The nationalistic, post-colonial and other mainstream literary criticism is inadequate to relate the lives, arts and cultures of the dalits.

While the coloniser attempted to modernise, develop and democratise the social institutions, which had benefitted the cream of the social strata, the native oppressor in India excluded the marginal from both organised and unorganised systems and institutions. The Indian forms of subordination and marginalisation dehumanised and obliterated the knowledge and identity of the marginal. Therefore even the post-colonial theory cannot account for the Indian forms of marginalisation and subordination.

The critiques and theoretical models of representations provided by Aime Cesaire, Frantz Fanon, Edward Said, Chinua Achebe, among others cannot be applied to the Indian forms of subordination, which differ from those of the rest of the postcolonial countries. The colonial practices of the binary thought, as Edward Said enunciated, produced the dichotomies—white-black, knowledge-ignorance, civilisation-barbarian, enlightenment-and so on: the former that of the European and the latter Asian, African and Latin American. Said contested the European dichotomisation. The same dichotomies have been in practice in India through the practice of caste. The post-colonial binariness cannot describe the synchronic nature of the caste, and therefore it cannot account for what may be termed the sub-marginal.

Basically concerned with the reversing of the historical center/margin, the discourses of the specificities critique the metropolis and the elite aesthetics emerging the theory from the marginal writings. The discourses of the marginal as a discipline begin where the Indian post-colonial theory ends.

The dalit studies, drawing from Ambedkar's socio-political philosophy, pursues the inclusion of the socially marginalised groups and their writings in the mainstream canon and discourse. By offering a fundamental critique of the Hindu ideology and upper caste domination, the studies seek to undo the hierarchical structuring and structural inequalities. Activist and adversarial in its approach, the writings of the marginal bring fresh perspectives on the productive culture in reconstructing nationalism by dismantling the exclusivist nationality.

The emergence of the dalit theory and political praxis, as attempts at centralising the margins, needs to be understood as responses to the failure of the reformative, nationalist and leftist movements, which had been led by the upper castes. Phule offered a challenge to Hinduism, at a time when Hinduism was in its heyday; his challenge had been a response to the collapse of the late nineteenth century Hindu reform movement. Following Phule, Ambedkar's social philosophy and political praxis had been a response to the nationalist movement and the post-independence left, both exclusivist in representation and ideology. In the contemporary times, Ambedkarism, coupled with the increasing globalisation of culture and multinational capitalism, is obliterating the remnant forms of the exclusivist practices.

Therefore, the suppressed traditions and the individual identity in India needed different theoretical models and new interpretive strategies for understanding the dalit/sudra and other marginalised traditions that have been historically obliterated by the elite cultures. Ambedkar's radicalised discourses explored the historical condition of dalit subordination. His works and praxis inaugurated the dalit activism and theory, including a new approach to literature beginning the second half of the twentieth century. The base of the new approach has been the argument that the notion of Indianness was constructed by the vedic scriptures to dominate sudras/dalits.

Continuing the legacy of critiques provided by Ambedkar, Gail Omvedt, Eleanor Zelliot, Kancha Ilaiah, Gopal Guru, Anand Teltumbde, Sukhdeo Thorat and others and the electoral strategy of Kansiram-Mayavati duo, theoretically facilitated the 'return of Ambedkar' in the last decade of the century creating socio-political space and agency hitherto denied to the marginalised communities.

Dalit writing therefore needs to go beyond the 'visible' dalits and pursue the inclusion of the cultures of the invisible communities. The castes—sub-castes and other castes—which are not a part of the organised and unorganised institutions need to be academicised. There is a need to offer a fundamental critique of the ideology and domination of not only the mainstream intellectuals but also that of the elites within the margins. The theory has to undo the 'imaginative liberation' of the sub-marginal. Just as the class based theory failed to obliterate conceptual as well as economic divides between the rich and the poor, the theory of the marginals cannot liberate the sub-marginal castes. The new theory, therefore, has to bring fresh perspectives to the role of intellectuals and political activists in the liberation of those, who are theoretically intractable. While the dalit theory emerged in the historical moment following the collapse of the reformative, nationalist and leftist discourses, the increasing divide between the marginal and the sub-marginal castes suggests a continued relevance of theorising the margins in the field of inquiry.

Dalit writing would encapsulate radicalisation of dalit consciousness, archive of fiction, poetry, polemical tracts, alternative history of Indian literature, social, economic and political contexts of dalit activism and writing the histories of land debates. The theory has to be firmly grounded in myth, politics, unknown and unseen material of the dalits with a contestation and negotiation of perspectives from below. The dalit studies emphasise the relationship of cultural identity to individual identity in historical circumstances. The studies have to explore new interpretive strategies for understanding the traditions of dalit sub-castes that have been historically marginalised by dominant cultures. With the cultural affirmation of what was marginalised, the dalit studies attract the intelligentsia demanding the unrestricted right to self-affirmation.

The dalit writing needs to address matters of identity, gender, exploitation and developing dalit nationalism based on productive culture. The theory needs to contest the notion that the marginals mimic the Sanskrit works, and that they are passive recipients of power. As Foucault would argue concerning the anti-colonial resistance, the struggles of the marginal accompany every deployment of power.

There is a need for broadening the scope of the writing of the marginal by conceiving dalit writing as new humanism privileging the human experience as central and fundamental; comparing the new humanism in terms of cross-cultural humanism; defining and formulating aesthetics as against the privileged mainstream literature; exploring the theme of humanising the dalits through literacy, education and empowerment. The essays in this volume are an attempt at the alternative historiography of regional writing with an analysis of the literary genres of Telugu dalit writing.

For Michel Foucault, the truth is not fixed; it changes: "the truth is never the same; there can be truth only in the form of the other world and the other life" (356). Truth, changing with new learning, with new experiences, is historical. The truth of aesthetics too is historical and ever changing, especially with challenges from counter-narratives. The concept of beauty also changes. Indian aesthetics guided by the *rasa* and *dhwani* theories has been resistant to change. With the emergence of new writing in India, the notion of aesthetics changed opening new ways of reading literature. The dalit writing, as other new literatures, serves a means of 'unconcealment or disclosure of the concealed state of things,' to use Heidegger's notion of truth. Dalit writing and aesthetics 'unconceal' by questioning the established practice of writing and reading. The dalit aesthetics marks change in the critical and political agenda for it not only revises its previously known parameters, but can be taken as suggesting new tasks dalit writing is to perform in a new historical context. In this sense, dalit aesthetics is a gesture towards reinventing dalit studies as well as a call for broadening the scope of Indian literature.

The concept of dalit aesthetics emanates from negating writing. Experiential in nature, it is primarily concerned with the problematic of representation, and in the existing terminology, may be characterised as *anubhava*. Before the emergence of the dalit writing, dalits were written about, which is speculation-based, *anumana*. The former concerns itself with the 'lived experience' and latter is primarily 'imaginary' or 'witnessed' experience. The representation of the dalits by the Indian English novelists, who are non-dalits, is a precursor to the emergence of a new genre, Dalit Writing in English. The representation of the dalits in English writing, and also other art forms like films and painting, are by typology, more acceptable because of the canonical advantages. The dalit representation needs to be examined from the dalit perspective with a focus on the question of authenticity and representation.

In its attempt to reclaim cultural space, dalit writing played an important role in articulating protest, self-respect, angst, identity, dignity, critiquing religion, politics, patriarchy and dalit patriarchy. Attacking traditional icons and symbols, writers created alternative icons. With the maturing of dalit writing in the last two decades, there have been attempts at drawing from alternative literary, cultural and religious sources. By doing so, contemporary dalit writers are now markedly deviating from the established norms, styles and techniques of mainstream writing. Fiction, imagination and romanticisation in prose writings are replaced by documentary kind of narratives, blurring the distinction between realism and fiction. Stylised syntax, pretentious diction and standardised styles have now made room for dialect and sociolect, which have earned respectability. Folk theatre forms are now resources for prose narratives. Hindu icons, imagery and value systems are now being replaced by dalit deities, rural imagery and upturned value system. The notion of beauty and truth has undergone a drastic change now, privileging the individual and his/her felt experiences rather than an abstract notion of imaginary beauty and archetypal experiences.

There is, however, criticism that dalit writing has run out of fuel, and is repeating itself. This could be perhaps due to dalit writers' lack of creation/recreation of dalit icons. Dalit *purnas* and sudra caste puranas are not being deployed in opposition to the iconic, canonical puranas of Hinduism. Dalits and sudra writers are yet to grow to accept each other's cultural history and tradition. Besides, the dependent dalit castes with rich cultural resources have the capacity to enrich dalit writing. Several studies in the last decade have been devoted to the thematic concerns of dalit writing, but not form and technique.

Dalit aesthetics pursues the inclusion of socially marginalised groups and their writings into the mainstream discourse. By offering a fundamental critique of the canonical forms of aesthetics, studies in dalit aesthetics seek to undo the hierarchical structuring bringing fresh perspectives in reconstructing literary discourses. The emergence of the dalit aesthetics needs to be understood as responses to the failure of the reformative, nationalist and leftist writings. This calls for different theoretical models and new interpretive strategies for understanding the tribal, dalit, sudra and other marginalised literatures.

Dalit aesthetics, therefore, needs to go beyond questioning canonical aesthetics and pursue the inclusion of the cultures of the invisible (dependent) castes. The castes—sub-castes and other castes—which are not a part of the organised and unorganised institutions need to be academicised. There is a need to offer a fundamental critique of the ideology and domination of not only the mainstream intellectuals but also that of the elites within the margins.

Therefore emerging dalit aesthetics would entail radicalisation of dalit consciousness, archive of fiction, poetry, polemical tracts, alternative history of Indian literature, social, economic and political contexts of dalit activism and writing. Dalit aesthetics address matters of identity, gender, exploitation and developing dalit nationalism based on productive culture. The theory needs to contest the notion that the marginals mimic the Sanskrit works, and that they are passive recipients.

There is a need for broadening the scope of the writing of the marginal by conceiving dalit writing as new humanism privileging the human experience as central and fundamental; comparing the new humanism in terms of cross-cultural humanism; defining and formulating aesthetics as against the privileged mainstream literature; exploring the theme of humanising dalits through literacy, education and empowerment. The discussion of Telugu dalit writing in different genres is presented in this volume in terms of innovations of aesthetics—the style and the technique

Reference

Michel Foucault. *The Courage of Truth: The Government of Self and Others II*. Trans. Graham Burchell. Hampshire (England): Palgrave Macmillan, 2011. Print.

Introduction

Of the fifteen hundred years of literary history, dalits were written about positively only in the last three hundred years. The mystic poets, Potuluri Veerabrahmam, a sudra social reformer, Yogi Vemana, a non-brahmin mystic, and the nineteenth century brahmin social reformers wrote against the untouchability, though within their limitations. By the twentieth century, dalits grew from the state of being written about to writing themselves, for above hundred years now. Continuing the tradition set by the pre-independence dalit writers, the contemporary writers, with their new voices, internationalised dalit writings making the genre respectable in cultural and academic spaces. This essay seeks to chart important landmarks in the evolution of dalit writing.

Telugu poetic movements, *bhava kavitvam* (romantic poetry), sickeningly subjective and *navya sampradaaya kavitvam* (neoclassical poetry), fanatically preoccupied with the revival of traditionalism, got de-linked from the contemporary socio-political reality. Jashuva, the first modern Telugu dalit poet known for his outstanding work, *Gabbilam* (The Bat) radicalised the Telugu writing by questioning the self-serving writers.

In the post-Independence period, the complaisant mainstream writers were bombarded by six *Digambara Kavulu*, (naked poets), Cherabandaraju, Bhairavaiah, Jwalamukhi, Nagnamuni, Nikhileshwar and Mahaswapna. They provided the much-needed jolt to the Telugu literature by re-linking literature to society. Their concerns being poverty, unemployment and political indifference, they made news about launching their anthologies: their first anthology was released in 1965 at a street-corner meeting by Nampalli Pandu, a rickshaw puller; the second in 1966 by Jangala Chitti, a hotel servant; the third, which had kick-started the modern Telugu literature, was dedicated in 1968 to Kanchikarla Kotesh, a dalit who was burnt alive by the upper castes accusing him of theft. This incident could be considered the forerunner to the identity movements, of dalit, feminist and *adivasi*, in times to come. For about the following two decades, the leftist organisations, drawing dalits into their cadre, undertook movements with a slogan, *dunne vadide bhoomi* (land for the tenants), which however did not benefit dalits, who have been only farmhands/labourers but not tenants.

1985, a landmark year in Andhra Pradesh, saw important developments concerning dalits: it was in this year the notorious Karamchedu massacre took place. Karamchedu is a village in Prakasham district of Andhra Pradesh, where six dalits were killed and three dalit women were raped by the forward caste men on July 17, 1985; seventeen dalits were massacred at Chundur on August 6, 1991; in between a minimum of twenty six of such incidents of murder or large scale arson took place killing a total of fifty seven dalits and setting on fire four hundred and thirty houses of the dalits, as explained by Balagopal. 'Dalit Mahasabha,' a social outfit, was founded to fight for the dalit rights; K.G. Satyamurthy, having challenged the leadership of the People's War (ML), resigned to his Central Committee membership accusing the Party of being casteist, and became an Ambedkarite effecting a shift in the debate from class to caste. A series of atrocities took place at Neerukonda, Thimma Samudram, Chundur, Vempenta and Cherlapally in the subsequent period. The pro and anti-reservation agitations—the BC reservation agitation, 1986 and the OBC (Mandal reservation), 1990—helped the dalits rally support and express solidarity for the dalit agitations. As a result, a spurt of dalit activities, ranging from literary and journalistic discourses to cultural and political forms of protest, had begun. The educated second generation dalits, who were the products of Ambedkar's thought, waged socio-political movements and agitations for self respect, civil rights, equality and empowerment of dalits.

Young dalits began to produce a powerful body of writing. In 1995, the first anthology of Telugu dalit poetry, *Chikkanavutunna Paata* (thickening song) was edited by G. Laxminarsaiah and Tripuraneni Srinivas, followed by *Padunekkina Paata* (sharpened song) edited by G. Laxminarsaiah (1996). Both the anthologies, though not exclusively dalit, are concerted efforts on the part of the poets and the anthologists to foreground dalit ethos, angst, protest, heritage, myth and an alternative vision. Some of the dalit poets in the anthologies emerged with new voices showing direction to the young and emerging dalit poets, who later on brought out a number of anthologies and published in the little magazines, which served as platforms for new debates.

Subordinating the Language

The dalit art and aesthetic had been subordinated at various stages in different guises though. Sambasiva Rao writes, dalits are considered *adi-dravidians*, the original inhabitants (36). An academy award winning dalit poet, Boyi Bheemanna attributed, according to Ganumula, the authorship of the Hindu scriptures to the dalits. The Aryans in the subsequent period subordinated the dravidians and imposed on them their language and culture. This was the beginning of the suppression of the dravidian language and art forms. The remnant forms of the original Telugu that might have existed during the non-Hindu periods like Budhism and the Jainism were suppressed. The native idiom was suppressed, and subsequently the Sanskritised Telugu was institutionalised under the patronage of the Telugu kings like Rajaraja Narendra of the eleventh century continuing up to the sixteenth century.

What the translator-poets had done was to transliterate the Sanskrit texts into Telugu script by affixing the case endings, *du*, *mu*, *vu* and *lu*. These poets include the eleventh century Nannaya, the first of the troika, who translated the

Mahabharath; the twelfth century Ketana who translated Dandi's *Dasakumara Charitra*; the fourteenth century Hulakki Bhaskarudu who translated Valmiki's *Ramayana*; the fifteenth century Sreenadha who translated *Srungara Naisadham*; and Potana who translated Vyasa's *Mahaabhagavatam*. These translations were not understood by dalits and sudras due to predominant Sanskrit elements. C.P. Brown (1798-1884), an English officer, and oriental lexicographer, observes that the "Sanskrit speech has influenced the Telugu language as much as, if not more than, Latin has influenced English" (Brown v). This only helped enliven the Sanskrit tradition in literature. Even after the emergence of the Telugu prose as the medium of literature, there have been writers using pedantic and Sanskritised Telugu. Chinnaya Suri (1807-1861), for instance wrote *Nitichandrika* (1853), the Telugu counterpart of *Panchatantra* in pedantic and plodding Telugu that is quite unreadable by ordinary readers. Ranga Rao, who brought out two volumes of Telugu short stories in English translation, observes that the pedantic style of Chinnaya Suri "affected literary Telugu, setting it back by at least fifty years. And the Telugu short story too has suffered" (258).

The brahmin writers suppressed Telugu disguisedly by extolling the kings in lieu of the patronage they had received in the form of *agraharams*, gift-villages, which continued through the fourteenth and fifteenth centuries. As a result, argues Chinna Rao, either the "society or the societal aspects of life was never the subject or the object of literature" (28) until the sixteenth century, dalits and sudras were not represented by the upper castes. If represented, dalits figured only negatively as demons and sinners in the Sanskrit epics. These forms of subordination have been questioned by different agencies at different points of time culminating in the dalit challenge.

Bhakti Writings

The first form of challenge was by the mystic poets. The non-brahmin mystics, Potuluri Veerabrahmam, Siddaiah and Yogi Vemana attempted at the reformation of dalits and sudras. They visited dalit and sudra streets educating them of self-respect, social equality and against the untouchability. The three of them became popular because of their social mission of educating, and liberating the masses from the clutches of social subordination. In the subsequent period, their writings as well as their lives had been subjected to obliteration. For example, Veerabrahmam, who became a cult figure, was said to have committed *sajiva samadhi*, burying alive. The dalit intellectuals in the modern period challenge that he might not have committed sajiva samadhi; the upper castes people, who could not digest his popularity, might have buried him alive or forced him bury himself. Similarly, Vemana, who questioned the brahmin hegemony, was dubbed as mad.

The mystics' writings and preaching were either made unavailable or misinterpreted. C.P. Brown edited and recorded for the posterity, the lost verses of Vemana. He served the Telugu language by recording in his dictionaries even the 'lowest' element of Telugu extant in the ancient dravidians. He had to depend upon the local educated brahmins, who worked as his scribes for tracing out and recording the mystics' poetry, especially Vemana's. In the process, the brahmin scribes had either suppressed or misinterpreted the mystics. What is available today could be either what had escaped the eye of the brahmin scribes.

The mystics' poetry led to a drastic change in Telugu language and literature. For the first time, the untouchables became the subject of literature written by the mystics, who undertook reformation around the same time in other parts of the country. They include Nandanar, a Shaivite poet of eighth century from Tamil Nadu; Tiruppan, a Vaishnavite of the same period; Chokkamela, a Mahar of the fourteenth century from Maharashtra; Ravidas, a Chamar (cobbler) of the fifteenth century from the North; and Kabir from Varanasi from Hindu Muslim background, criticised the untouchability. Since Hinduism as a religion has been averse to reformation and modernisation, the mystics attempted to reform the society by questioning the basis of social inequality and discrimination. Vemana questioned various socio-cultural aspects of the orthodoxies. Apart from Vemana, other mystics, who wrote poetry with a reformative mission against the practice of caste system and untouchability include Chandidas in Bengali; Kabir in Hindi; Nanak in Punjabi; and Sarvagna in Kannada. A tradition thus started by the bhakti writers was to suffer a break in the subsequent times.

Social Reformation

After a protracted hiatus for about two hundred years, caste and untouchability were talked about in the nineteenth century social reformation. Gurajada Appa Rao (1862–1915) and Kandukuri Veereshalingam (1848-1919) championed the concerns of women, especially upper castes and brahmins. The reformation movement expanded its scope to educating people against social evils like untouchability, child marriages, bride-money, caste, widow remarriages and religious hatred. Gurajada used the short story for propagating the reforms in the society. To suit his need, Gurajada deviated from the established literary tradition regarding themes and language: the themes of his stories were didactic; and the language he preferred was the spoken mode. The first version of his famous story, "Diddubatu" was written in semi-classical style. Later on, he revised it in the spoken idiom making it easily intelligible. Gurajada and Kandukuri "broadened the base and scope of literature as well as transformed the traditional character of Telugu literature into the modern tool of communication" (Ramakrishna 71). The reformers used the short story for propagating the reformation. In a way the credit for modernising the Telugu literature goes to the social reformers. Therefore, Gurajada is considered the harbinger of modernity in Telugu literature.

There were, however, certain limitations to the reformation movement. The reformers did not question the socio-religious bases that sanctified the evil practices. The social reformers failed to come to terms with the basic tenets and framework of the Hinduism. Their attempts were aimed at reforming select evil practices. They did not question and negate the caste system. The social reformers of the modern Andhra did not continue the medieval bhakti tradition. There was a break. The social reformation must be understood as a reaction to the incorporation of dalits into the Christianity and the missionary education of the Europeans. The most conspicuous aspect of questioning the caste and the concomitant evils like the untouchability, discrimination and oppression were absent in the most famous literary works of Gurajada Apparao's play *Kanyasulakam* (1892) and Veereshalingam's novel *Rajasekhara Charitam* (1880), the first Telugu novel.

The Dalit Challenge

The subordination of the dalits had been challenged in various forms though it did not take the shape of sustained movement. The seventeenth century bhakti movement being the first organised challenge, the second one was the nineteenth century social reformation movement and the third and the most decisive challenge, this time by dalits, was the Adi-Andhra movement. The first conference having taken place in 1917, the Adi-Andhra movement held a series of conferences and public meetings under the leadership of Bhagya Reddy Verma. In the subsequent period the movement took different forms in the names of Adi-Andhra and Adi-Dravida movements. Bhagya Reddy Verma played a pivotal role in radicalising and organising the dalits.

As a part of this movement, Kusuma Dharmanna wrote against caste oppression, untouchability and discrimination. He stressed that the dalits were the original inhabitants, and demanded that the term 'Adi-Andhra' be used to refer to them. The aspirations of the dalits were reflected in the writings of the first generation dalit writers in the 30s and 40s. Boyi Bheemanna demanded unity between mala and madiga, whom he termed the *ma-ma* castes. He claimed the highest order of the dalits being the descendants of Arundhati and Vasistha against the lowest. Another dalit writer, Jala Rangaswami denounced the Aryan conquest that enslaved the dalits, and wrote about the glory of the pre-Aryan past. The poets of this generation were vociferous in attacking the brahminical order. Thus, following the bhakti tradition, and the limited appeal of the social reformation movement, the dalit intellectuals played a vital role in radicalising the dalit thought and polity. In this regard, a noted historian, Adapa Satyanarayana writes, “The dalit intellectuals of the pre-Independence period were the forerunners to the contemporary dalit literary and cultural movements in the state” (Satynarayana 94).

After a volatile dalit activism during 1900-1930, the Congress party suppressed the dalit struggles in the name of nationalist movement. This may be understood as a form of the hegemony of the upper castes. The dalit movement had to give in to the forces with the death of Bhagya Reddy Verma in 1939. In the following period, both the Congress and the Communists successfully diverted the issue from the dalit question: the Congress used dalits as the vote-bank, and the left used the dalits as its cadre in the name of struggle for lands. By 1950s the dalit movement almost came to an end for want of leadership, never to recover till the 1980s. There had been a lull in the activities especially during the Nationalist period.

The dalit struggles and their challenge of subordination were not represented in the literature of the upper castes. The early leaders of the nationalist movement, Tanguturi Prakasham, Pattabhi Seetharamaiah and Burgula Ramakrishna Rao, too privileged the translation literature leading to the destruction of the unique Teluguness and culture. Telugu was considered the language of dalits and sudras, a phenomenon comparable to English which had been considered the language of the poor during the formative years of English language. English was considered a language of the poor and working classes in England. The status of English changed only when Henry IV made it England’s Official language. English was allowed as a subject after a great deal of resistance in 1894 in Oxford; 1911 in Cambridge. Charles Grant recommended the introduction of English as the medium of instruction in 1772, almost a hundred years prior to its being recognised by the Oxford and the Cambridge Universities. Till then English was treated only a dialect. The established writers during the nationalist period continued to depart from dalit tradition. The nationalistic literature did not reflect dalit and sudra life. The nationalist leaders believed that national liberation would liberate dalits too. Unnava Laxminarayana's novel, *Malapalli* (1922) and N. G. Ranga's *Harijana Nayakudu* (1933) represent this dimension. The Gandhian agenda of the 'Harijan upliftment' was criticised by dalit writers like Jala Rangaswami.

Similarly the progressive literature of the 1940s too sought to sideline the socio-cultural specificities like caste, gender and ethnicity. Marxists failed to understand the caste specific character of the Indian society. Kancha Ilaiah makes an interesting observation regarding the dalit ascendancy to political power that a few dalit leaders emerged as leaders especially in the Congress, but not among Communists, who claim to struggle for the empowerment of the oppressed. Damodaram Sanjivayya of the Congress was made the first chief minister of Andhra Pradesh in 1960; he was also the first dalit to be the president of the AICC. However it was a different story that dalits could not serve their people in spite of the political ascendancy. The liberation of the dalits was not on the agenda of the social reformers, nationalist fighters and leftists. It is in this context that Gail Omvedt explains why the Phule-Ambedkar movement had been overshadowed by the politics of the left and the right. The nationalist movement was idealised as inclusivist by the nationalist historians who saw the pre-Independence history "only in terms of political opposition to a foreign power" (Omvedt 16).

Untouchability within Untouchability

Untouchability within untouchability is the unique inhuman aspect of the caste system practiced in India. While the madiga are untouchable to the mala, the madiga treat certain other sub-castes untouchable to them. The madiga constitute the main supporting caste to certain other dependent castes. T.R. Singh terms them the 'central caste' and the 'satellite castes' respectively. He explains, "the main supporting caste has been called central caste; the others economically dependent upon, but complementing the socio-cultural life of the former, have been satellites" (Singh 93).

Varying from region to region, there are several castes, who depend on the madiga. The names and nature of these castes differ from region to region. Some of the common satellite castes include dakkali, chindu, baindla, erpula, madiga-mastin, kommuvaru, binedu, jambava, matangi and pambala. They remain at the periphery of the caste system; at the periphery of the madiga wadas. Each of the dependent castes has a specific and specialised role to play so as to depend on the madiga. Therefore, they are considered professional groups since they are identified with a particular profession, which is directly or indirectly connected to the madiga but not to the rest of the castes in the village. They do not form part of the village in any respect.

The dakkali, for instance are the beggars of the madiga; they beg from the madiga during the harvest days. They are one of the most detested castes among the dalit castes. Considered inferior, the dakkali are not even allowed to enter the madiga wadas and they are assigned lower status in the madiga hierarchy. The madiga consider the dakkali 'half-caste' and not a 'full-caste' meaning the dakkali caste is not incorporated into the village or the caste system, and they have no particular occupation or service to render to the upper castes. Interestingly, such a mean caste is assigned a culturally important occupation: they are the custodians of madiga's legendary lore. They sing songs in praise of the madiga.

Some of the other satellite castes include the chindu, who stage dramatic scenes from the epics, the *Ramayan* and the *Mahabharath* for the madiga as well as the rest of the people in the village. The chindu spare a woman for the madiga, who use her as a collective wife, and worship her as goddess Yellamma; the baindla discharge priestly functions to the madiga and perform religious rites to the music of *Jamadika*, a musical instrument characteristic of their occupation; the madiga-mastin beg the madiga by playing on a particular musical instrument.

The mala, who treat madiga untouchable, have been in the forefront in socio-political and economic ascendancy. The fertile lands, irrigation facilities, exposure to the British rule, the Missionary education, health and the Church, helped the mala of the coastal region in their upward mobility. In contrast, the madiga outnumber the mala in the Telangana region, which was under the feudal regime reeling under economic backwardness and social oppression. The madiga lag far behind the mala in literacy, employment and politics. The writings of the mala concomitantly dominated those of the madiga. The mala writers, Kusuma Dharmanna, Gurram Jashuva, Boyi Bheemanna and Jala Rangaswamy (all from the coastal region) made name while their madiga counter parts, Dunna Iddak, Vemulapalli Devendar, were rather unknown. The first madiga writer to be acclaimed has been Kolakaluri Enoch, who initially was more of an outward looking writer, and he asserted his madiga identity, and became an inward looking writer after the Dandora movement.

Madiga writers, since the nineties, have been vocal, pungent and influential. Some of them include Yendluri Sudhakar, Vemula Yellaiah, Nagappagari Sunderraju and the madiga women writers include Gogu Shyamala, Jupaka Subhadra and Jajula Gowri, who exemplified through their writings that the writers from the below narrate the stories of exclusion, suffering and rebellion and their aspirations for freedom, dignity and equality. The madiga writings enlivened Telugu dalit writing when the Telugu dalit literature was about to repeat itself.

The contemporary madiga writers represent the dependant castes too. The baindla, erpula, dakkali and chindu have been written about by madiga. Just as the dalits had been written about by the upper castes from 1910 to 1940s, the dependant castes have been written about by the madiga since 2000. The dependant castes are yet to write themselves: they still need to grow from being written about to writing themselves. The Telugu dalit writing, in this respect, has a long way to go.

The Dandora movement led by Krishna Madiga has been a step in this direction. The Dandora movement has been relentlessly fighting for the sub-classification of the dalit castes, which was legally questioned on technical grounds. The movement is however successful in terms of identity and self-respect. The term, 'madiga' used to be derogative attracting the atrocities Act. A term associated with filthiness is now being suffixed, becoming a symbol of identity and self-respect. This is a symbolic achievement of the Dandora movement.

References

Balagopal, K. "Post-Chundur and Other Chundurs." *Economic and Political Weekly* (October 19, 1991). Print.

Brown, C.P. "Introduction." *Dictionary: Telugu-English*, New Delhi: Asian Educational Services, 1986. Print.

Ganumala, Gnaneshwar, ed. *Boyi Bhimanna Sahiti Sastipurti Sanchika*. Hyderabad: Sahiti Sastipurti Prachurana, 1983. Print.

Ilaiah, Kancha. "Caste or Class or Caste-Class: A Study in Dalit Bahujan Consciousness in Andhra Pradesh in 1980s." History and Society: Research in Progress Papers, New Delhi: NMML, 1995. Print.

Jashuva, Gurram. *Gabbilam*, Trans. by K. Madhava Rao, Hyderabad: Jashuva Foundation,1996. Print.

Laxminarsaiah, G. and Tripuraneni Srinivas. *Chikkanavutunna Paata.* Vijayawada: Kavithvam Prachuranalu, 1995. Print.

Laxminarsaiah, G. *Padunekkina Paata*. Vijayawada: Dalit Sana Prachuranalu, 1996. Print.

Omvedt, Gail. *Dalits and the Democratic Revolution: Dr. Ambedkar and the Dalit Movement in Colonial India.* Delhi: Sage, 1994. Print.

Ramakrishna, V. "Literary and Theater movements in Colonial Andhra: Struggle for Left Ideological Legitimacy." *Social Scientist*, Vol. 21, Nos. 1-2.1993. Print.

Ranga Rao, "Afterword." *Classic Telugu Short Stories.* New Delhi: Penguin Books, 1995. Print.

Rao, Sambasiva. "Panchamula Pracheenatha." *Andhra Patrika Ugadhi*

Sanchika, cited in Chinna Rao, Yagati, *Dalits' Struggle for Identity*. New Delhi: Kanishka Publishers, 2003. Print.

Satyanarayana, A. *Dalits and Uppercastes: Essays in Social history*. New Delhi: Kanishka Publishers, 2005. Print.

1

Social Movements and Identity Formation

The Roots

The roots of identity movements may be traced in Buddhism, Bhakti movements and social reformation movements culminating in the contemporary identity movements. The transformation of social movements into identity formation has been an outcome of the intellectualisation of the former by Phule and Ambedkar, among others. This paper seeks to examine the role of the social movements in the formation of the Dalit identity.

The Bakti saints made a remarkable contribution in the form of questioning the hegemony. The Bhakti challenge, during the 10th and 13th centuries, of the religious restrictions on worship became popular among the sudras and Dalits. The Bhakti movement helped construct an identity in opposition to the Brahmin identity. The mystics who led the Bhakti movement include Ramanand and Ravidas in the North, Chaitanya and Chandidasa in the east, Eknath, Choka Mela, Tukaram and Narsinh Mehta in the west and Ramanuja, Nimbaraka and Basava in the south. Their contribution to the anti-Brahmin thought lies in opposing caste distinctions and asserting equality before god. M.G. Ranade called the Bakti movement being unbrahminical (cited in Mani 169). However, the saint poets did not advocate detachment from normal worldly life as a prerequisite for the salvation. They advocated normal family life in society. Unlike the Brahmin priests, Bakti poets disapproved renunciation, asceticism and celibacy as the means of enlightenment. The significant contribution of the Bakti poets is that the untouchables identified themselves as anti-Brahminical by which they formed a unique non-Brahmin identity.

Adi Movements

Next to the Bhakti movement, the 'Adi' movements were significant in the formation of the Dalit identity. Gail Omvedt argues that "The mobilisation of the oppressed and exploited sections of society the peasants, Dalit, women and low castes that Phule had spoken of as shudras and ati-shudras occurred on a large scale in the 1920s and 1930s, under varying leaderships and with varying ideologies" (Omvedt 34). The non-Aryan or the non-Brahmin movements in Maharashtra and Tamil Nadu, the Dalit movements in Punjab and Karnataka were against the Aryan conquest and Brahmin exploitation through religion and culture. These movements, being aimed at the argument of the original inhabitants, have a common tag 'Adi' which means original inhabitant. Most of the Dalit movements like 'Adi-Dharma' in Punjab, 'Adi-Hindu' in UP and Hyderabad, 'Adi-Dravida,' 'Adi-Andhra' and 'Adi-Karnataka' in South India have a common claim of the Dalits and sudras being the original habitants of India.

The Adi-Dharma movement, Led by Mangoo Ram in Punjab, made a substantial contribution to the social and political life of Dalits in Punjab. He was influenced by the Ghadar movement, a radical organisation in California aimed at liberating India from British rule through armed insurrection. He opened a school for the lower caste children in the village, where the Adi-Dharma movement was launched in 1926. The ideology and principles of the Adi-Dharma movement greatly influenced the Dalits of the Doaba region decisively contributing to the formation of the Dalit identity.

Adi-Hindu movement, under the leadership of Swami Acchutanand, in Uttar Pradesh is another significant movement that contributed to the construction of the Dalit identity in the 1920s. Though Arya Samaj promised to facilitate the social uplift of lower castes, its intention of enslaving untouchables to Hinduism is criticised by the Adi-Hindu leaders. Swami Acchutanand claimed in a speech, "The Samaj aimed to make all Hindus slaves of the Vedas and the Brahmins" (cited in Goopt 13).

Acchutanand and Ram Charan constructed an identity which traces out the history of the original inhabitants of India. They outlined an idealised vision of social equality and of past power and glory of the untouchables. Self-assertion was an important principle of Adi-Hindu movement. Exploring the identities of self-assertion and empowerment that Adi movements espoused, Nandini Goopt states that by asserting that the untouchables were the true masters of the land, the Adi-Hindu preachers cultivated a sense of entitlement to rights and power at the same time as they heightened an awareness of historical deprivation. The stress on *atmagyan* (self-knowledge) and introspection as the source of independent knowledge without higher caste impositions also enabled the exposition of a distinction, autonomous, proud and even defiant self-identity of the untouchables (Goopt 21).

The Adi-Hindu movement provided not only an ideology of radical equality and a strategy for doing better in everyday life, but also "a political culture for civil rights and organised protest" (Khare 78). Though the Arya Samaj and Congress have caused to split the Adi-Hindu movement in 1930s, the Adi-Hinduism, on the whole formed the dominant and sustained form of its political expression and a constructive identity.

The Adi movements in South India played their role in constructing Dalit identity. The untouchable movements in Nagpur, Adi Dravida movement in Tamil, Adi Karnataka movement in Mysore, Adi Andhra movement in Andhra Pradesh under Madras Presidency and Adi-Hindu movement under the

Nizam reign had paved the way for constructing the Dalit identity in South India.

Relatively a strong and independent Dalit movement grew in Nagpur with Kisan Faguji Bansode (1870-1946) as the leader. In 1903, he founded his first organisation in Mohapa, his village and many educational Institutions including a school for girls in 1907. Bansode wrote several books and started several papers. Later, many leaders especially Vithoba Ravji Moonpandit (1860-1924) and Ganesh Akkaji Gavai (1888-1974) came into light as the untouchable leaders. Ganesh Akkaji Gavai founded a Mahar Library and Mahar Sudharak Mandal in his village. Kalicharan Nandagawali (1886-1962) founding the first girls' school and also became a member of the legislative council.

EV. Rama Swamy (1879-1973) popularly known as Periyar led the self-respect movement in Tamil Nadu. One of the greatest anti-Brahmin movements in India, the self-respect movement targeted the Brahmin dominance criticising the idol worship. Aloysius comments in this regard: "His focus was not God and religion in general or in the philosophical sense but religion in particular – the Brahminical religion – taken in its practical – social dimension of buttressing up social iniquity and in humanity" (Aloysius, 4). All the religions being historical creations tend to accumulate beliefs and practices that become anachronistic and anti-social. Periyar clarifies that, "The self-respect movement was started with the objective of instilling a sense of self-respect in the people of this country and to unify them. The self-respect movement really endeavours in transparency, to explain why and how the people of our country had lost their self-pride, to assert that the obstacles in their way should be abolished and indeed to abolish such obstacles" (cited in Aloysius, 5).

Periyar educated the Dravidians and Adi-Dravidians to bring about a cultural revolt with an aim of making society casteless and egalitarian. Braj Ranjan Mani observes:

Stressing egalitarian social relations across caste, community and gender lines, Periyar advocated the overthrow of caste and instituted non-Brahminic forms of marriage celebrating the equality of women and her right to choose life-partner and other such practices designed to give a death blow to the Brahminical order. Presenting a radical critique of the religious beliefs and practices in a variety of ways, Periyar wanted to demolish the whole Brahminic structure of society which he saw as the root cause of the degradation and subordination of women and the non-brahmin populace (Mani 325).

Periyar joined the Congress in 1919 and became a prominent figure in Tamil Congress. But he left it to organise the self-respect movement. Periyar also disagreed with Gandhi on issues like caste, culture and nationalism.

Another prominent identity moment in Tamil Nadu was led by Jyothee Thaass, who campaigned for Dalits' education. He set up several schools for Dalits and his writings are remarkably modern for espousing the cause of social emancipating, Buddhism, rationalism and the new egalitarian Dravidian identity (Mani 314). He considered the Brahmins mentally, morally and culturally depressed as they clanged on to anachronistic beliefs and obscurantist practices.

Another significant movement of identity was organised in Kerala by Ayyankali, Pokayil Yohannan and Pamapady John Joseph. Sri Narayana Guru (1856-1928) was an active socio-political and religious reformer for nearly four decades during the most critical period of Kerala's history. He believed in the message of one god, one religion and one caste, which developed a new consciousness among the Dalits. The backward caste movements in Kerala differed from other movements like that of Jotirao Phuley, whose movement consisted of shudras, the untouchable and women. But such an attempt was absent in Kerala and the movement lead by Sree Narayana Guru remained mostly the movement for the upliftment and empowerment of the Izhavas.

Among the Dalit movements in Kerala, the movement by Ayyankali was of great success in constructing Dalit identity.

Ayyankali, an illiterate, unlike Sree Narayana Garu, was not philosophical. His movement was humanistic and democratic. To him, socio-cultural issues were more important than the economic issues. Ayyankali fought for the rights of his people to use public space. By doing so, Ayyankali successfully contributed to the formation of the individual identity.

Ayyankali established an open school in Vengannoor in 1904 but faced severe resistance from the caste Hindus. He gathered the scheduled castes to go on strike and continued it for one full year. To protect the strikers against criminal elements recruited by landlords, a small group of youth known as 'Ayyankali Pada' was formed under his organisation.

Another element that Ayyankali movement concentrated on was performing folk arts. Ayyankali collected small band of youth belonging to his caste and trained them in martial and folk arts like 'pattukachery', 'parijakali', 'kolkali', 'kurathiattom', 'kakkarassi drama' and 'valli drama.' This was his first attempt at identity construction.

Formation of Sadhu Jana Paripalana Sangam (SJPS) was another significant form of identity formation in the Ayyankali movement. It was democratic in character and gender sensitive. Kerala Pulayar Maha Sabha by TT Kesava Shashtri, son-in-law of Ayyankali, obtained the four basic rights for the Dalits: right to appear in pubic places decently dressed, right to education, cultural rights and the right to be represented in the government. These were the subtle forms of the assertion of the Dalit identiy.

The Dalit movements in Andhra Pradesh began as early as 1900. The Adi-Hindu movements in Hyderabad and Adi-Dravida movement in Andhra region played significant roles in constructing the Dalit identity in the pre-independent period. The Adi-Hindu movement under Nizam rule was led by Bagya Reddy Varma (1888-1939), who organised 'Jagan Mitra Mandali' in 1906, found Manya Samngam in 1911 and the Adi-Hindu organisation in the same year. Bagya Reddy Varma and his followers strongly fought for the compulsory education to the Dalit children. He opposed the practices like child marriages, eating meat and using drink in marriages and notions like Jogini, Murti and Basivi through which young and uneducated untouchable girls were devoted to gods and goddesses. Between 1906 and 1916, Bagya Reddy Varma's concentration was particularly on educating Dalits through folk songs and street plays. He went across the entire Telangana region and gave the message of revolution to the Dalits. Arige Ramaswami and B. Syam Sundhar were other contemporaries of Bagya Reddy Varma who contributed to the construction of Dalit identity in Hyderabad state.

The Adi-Andhra Movement took place in the coastal parts of Andhra Pradesh. The common interface between the Adi-Hindu Movement in Hyderabad and the Adi-Andhra Movement in Andhra was that both the movements were led by Bagya Reddy Varma. The Adi-Andhra movement began in 1917 with the 'First Provincial Panchama Mahajana Sabha' organised in Vijayawada. Bagya Reddy Varma opposed the use of the term *panchamas.*

The Adi-Andhra movement became a platform for political mobilisation. Boyi Bhimanna, Kusuma Dharmmanna and Jala Rangaswamy wrote against caste oppression, untouchability and discrimination. Gurram Jashuva's *Piradousi* (1932) and *Gabbilam* (The Bat); Kusuma Dharmanna's *Makoddee Nalla Dhoratham* (1933), *Harijana Shathakam* (1933), *Madhyapana Nishedham* (1930); Boyi Bhimanna's *Paleru* (1940), *Cooliraju* (1947) and *Jana Padhuni Jabhulu* (1940); Jala Rangaswami's *Mala Shuddi* (1930); Nakka China Venkataiah's *Harijana Keerthanalu* (1935) were among those who wrote about the Dalit identity.

Ambedkar

Following the mystics' and the social activists' attempts at crystallising the Dalit identity, Dr BR Ambedkar (1891-1956) provided intellectual basis to the formation of the Dalit identity. Ambedkar, organised Dalits socially, politically and intellectually through the process of which, the formation of the Dalit identity assumed a definitive form. Ambedkar launched many struggles during the 50 years of his social life. Ambedkar's Mahad struggle for the untouchable's access to public water in 1927 was successful as a civil rights issue. Ambedkar fought for separate electorates for the Dalits and emphasised that Dalits' identity is different from that of the Hindus. He even asked the Dalits to have their dwellings away from the Hindu Society. As the Chairman of the Drafting Committee and the first Law Minister, Ambedkar contributed immeasurably to the socio-cultural assertion of the dalit identity. With the embracing of Buddhism with many of his followers and in proclaiming Buddhism as the alternative to the irrational Hinduism, Ambedkar provided spiritual basis to the Dalit identity.

Jyothiba Phule's women liberation movement inspired Ambedkar. Liberation of the women was taken up by him as the main aspect of the renaissance. In addition to the Hindu reformist programmes of the widow marriages and annihilation of the *sati* system, he concentrated on education and rights for women. He struggled hard to liberate women from the age-old slavery and to create a share in all the spheres of life.

While Brahmo Samaj and Arya Samaj kept women in dark, Ambedkar opened up new horizons of freedom and equality for women. Instead of proposing reformations for women, he put forward total liberation for women. He awakened their mind, ignited their heart, strengthened their energies and resurrected them as powerful human beings. He fought against the state and society to realise justice for women.

The services rendered by Ambedkar to the liberation of women played important role in the enactment of laws. His relentless fight for bringing out revolutionary changes in the social and economic life of women in the form of introducing the Hindu Code Bill is important. On marriage, divorce and succession of parental properties, he proposed the abolition of polygamy and also the right of divorce to Hindu women and a share in the husband's and father's property.

The Dalit movements from 1980s onwards aimed at fighting for Dalit assertion. The exploitation and discrimination of the Dalits on one hand and their protest and revolt on the other hand initiated the questions of self-assertion and consciousness among the Dalits. Through their revolt, Dalits provided a new identity for them. This identity strengthened its resolve to fight every form of discrimination and determine the path for liberation. Asserting themselves, the Dalits challenged the very foundation on which the Indian society and polity are based.

Taking the lead from Ambedkar's theoretical basis of the Dalit identity, literary writers and activists began to narrate the Dalit experiences. Dalit writers and activists brought awareness among the Dalits. The concerns of the writers include denial of access to resources, participation in political processes, exclusion from social institutions, construction of Dalit identity, demanding equal share in resource, among others. Their writings are aimed at building awareness.

Conclusion

The Dalit writers being the victims, they use literature as a vehicle to propagate the Ambedkarite ideology. The Dalit literature, written in all the genres like short stories, novels, poetry, critical essays, plays and autobiographies, provides critical insights into the question of the Dalit identity. The teachings of Ambedkar sharpened their sensitivities, and made them outward-looking, articulate and assertive in their expression. The Dalit writings are used to educate the Dalits. The prose narratives, especially mediated between Dalit writers and the Dalits to form the modes of social protest. The dalit narratives are used to raise awareness that caste is the root cause of social discrimination. The Dalit narratives capture the local idiom finding global space. Subverting the conventional epistemology, Dalit writers challenge the Brahminism through their writings.

References

Aloysius, G. *Periyar on Islam.* New Delhi: Critical Quest, 2004. Print.

Goopt, Nandini. *Swami Acchutanand and The Adi-Hindu Movement.* New Delhi: Critical Quest, 2006. Print.

Khare, R. S. *The Untouchable as Himself: Ideology, Identity and Pragmatism among the Lucknow Chamars.* Cambridge, 1984. Print.

Mangoo Ram, Ronki Ram. *Ad Dharm and The Dalit Movement in Punjab.* New Delhi : Critical Quest, 2008. Print.

Mani, Braj Ranjan. *Debrahminising History : Dominance and Resistance in Indian Society.* New Delhi : Monetary, 2005. Print.

Omvedt, Gail. *Dalit Visions: The Anti-Caste Movement and the Construction of an Indian Identity,* New Delhi : Orient Longman, 2006. Print.

2

Movement Literature: A Dalit Critique

I

The tradition of movement literature in Telugu may be traced back to Bhakti movement. Beginning from the bhakti movement in the seventeenth century, the movements—social reformation, adi, progressive, digambara poetry, revolutionary, feminist, dalit and Telangana—have inalienable link with Telugu literature. Most of the activists who participated in the movements were themselves literary writers. The activist-writer relationship is so inalienable that the two-way influence is comparable to the African/black writing that produced Ngugi Wa Thiango, Dennis Brutus, Benjamin Jephaniah, to name only a few. This article seeks to examine (a) the role and status of the dalits in the movement literature; and (b) the elite writers' attitude and world views vis-à-vis dalits and their writing during different literary movements.

In its fifteen hundred years of literary history, the dalit writing has been subjected to obliteration and stifling of their voices. The dalits were considered not worthy of being written about. If they had to figure in literature, they were portrayed only as demons, sinners, *chandalas*, *mlechas* because of the 'violation' of the principles laid in *puranas, sastras* and *Manusmrithi*. The instances of castigating and punishing the dalits abound in the epics as illustrated by Vijaya Bharathi. In the subsequent periods and literary movements, the dalit question is not addressed, and the proponents/manifestoes of the movements have been silent on the social configuration of oppression.

Bhakti Movement

Since the medieval period, the Telugu speaking region of the Deccan witnessed the development of the bhakti movement, the earliest one being Palkurki Somanatha (1160–1240), whose works could be considered a precursor to the reform movements and against orthodox practices. Atukuri Molla (1440-1530), whom Kancha Ilaiah considers the first feminist (8), wrote *Molla Ramayanam*, from Sita's perspective. A sudra woman belonging to *kummari*, potter, having been refused to be taught by a brahmin, chose a sudra teacher, learnt Telugu and Sanskrit and authored the epic differently from the existing versions. In the same lineage, Potuluri Veerabrahmam (1610-), a sudra mystic belonging to *avusula*, goldsmith, who was considered Nostradamus of India authored seven hundred verses, visited the villages along with his disciples to educate the people against the evil practices of the caste and religion. He might have been forced to commit *sajeeva samadhi*, entombing oneself by the intolerant upper castes. Born a hundred years after him was another mystic Vemana (1700–50), a non-brahmin mystic, who wrote *Vemana sathakam*, a rare genre in simple verse popularly reaching out to the commoners. Singing against the varna system, Vemana grew so popular that the upper castes branded him mad and obliterated most of his verses, some of which had been retrieved by C.P. Brown, an English officer who had learnt Telugu and compiled Telugu-English dictionaries.

The genres that the mystics wrote in were close to the illiterate masses—a radical departure from the unintelligible works written before and during the period of the mystic poets. The mystics emphasised in unequivocal terms the inequalities and injustices bequeathed by the *varna* system. The medieval bhakti tradition paid attention to the sufferings of those at the bottom of the caste hierarchy. Their writings and preaching were a reaction to the feudal order of the day: the mystics challenged the feudal order which the brahmins did not. A tradition from the below thus started in the medieval period, broke off in the ensuing modernist movements—the reform, nationalist, progressive, revolutionary, feminist and Telangana, excepting the adi and dalit movements.

Reform Movement (1905-1920)

The social reform movement, a result of the influence of the liberal Europe, suffered a limitation of being confined to select castes. While the bhakti movement was inclusivist, the reform movement had been self-consciously exclusivist: it excluded the reform of the sudras and ati-sudras, whose productive culture determined the nationality.

Commenced by Kandukuri Vireshalingam (1848–1919), the tradition of exclusion of the sudras and ati-sudras from the ambit of reformation, had been discursively continued by the other reformers including Gurajada Appa Rao (1862-1915), Raghupati Venkatratnam Nayudu (1862-1939) and Chilakamarthi Laxminarasimha Panthulu (1867-1945). Interestingly, the former two used literature as an effective means of disseminating the reformative message through *Rajasekhara Charitramu* (1880), the first social novel; and an influential play, *Kanyasulkam* (1892) respectively. However, a positive aspect is that being didactic in nature, the reformative writings "broadened the base and scope of literature transforming the traditional character of Telugu literature into a modern tool of communication" (Ramakrishna 71).

The beginnings of the Telugu short story coincided with the social reform movement. The writings of Gurajada and Vireshaligam focused mainly on such themes and problems as bride price and widow remarriage of the upper castes. However, none of their works, *Kanyasulkam* and *Raja Shekhara Charitramu*, being very popular, did not address the seminal problem of caste and the alienation of the sudras and ati-sudras from the mainstream society. Problems central to the varna system did not draw their attention. Their reading of classical texts and scriptures was only aimed at reforming some aspects of Hindu society, but not to question and negate the varna system.

The first limitation being exclusivist, the second limitation of the social reformers of modern Andhra is that it failed to inherit and continue the medieval bhakti tradition.

Adi-Movement (1906-1935)

The Adi movements were the first concerted dalit movements led by the dalits in Andhradesa and other parts of the country. They may be understood as a reaction to the failure of the reform movement in addressing the caste/dalit question. Bhagya Reddi Varma (1888-1939), the forerunner of the dalit social movement, founded Jagan Mitramandali in 1906, Manyasangham in 1911 and organised Adi–Andhra Mahasabha, which held its conferences between 1917 and 1938 in different parts of Andhra (Adi-Hindu movement was organised in Hyderabad and Telangana), which helped in the mobilisation of the dalits in the struggle for social emancipation. A writer, orator and organiser, Verma mobilised the dalits for self-respect and social equality movement. Other activists Sundru Venkataiah, B.S. Venkat Rao, Kusuma Dharmanna and Vemula Kurmaiah provided the leadership for dalit movement, the basic thrust of which was to critique the exploitative ideology and counter the socio-cultural hegemony of the upper castes.

The main focus of the movement was abolition of untouchability, caste oppression and discrimination, which were represented adequately in the literacy and cultural traditions of dalits in the 1930s and 1940s. The spread of education in the coastal Andhra by the Missionaries helped emerge writer-activists like Gurram Jashuva, Boyi Bheemanna, Kusuma Dharmanna, among many others. Each of them worked in his own way: Bhagya Reddy Varma believed that the panchamas, as they were called, had never been a part of the caste system; they were Adi-Andhras, the original inhabitants of the land. On the demand of the Adi-Andhra Mahasabha, the government designated them in the gazette as Adi-Andhras. Jala Ranga Swamy, in "Who are the

Untouchables" reasoned that the Panchamas were the original people. Defeating the Anarya rulers, the Aryan invaders subjugated them:

> *Some occupations were created and assigned to us*
>
> *we were named serfs*
>
> *caste discrimination was introduced*
>
> *we were suppressed*
>
> *we were troubled with slavery*
>
> *occupational differences were imposed*
>
> *we were alienated (*cited in *Satyanarayana 87)*

Great Poet, Gurram Jashuva too questioned the logic of the creation of the panchamas. Boyi Bheemanna, who coined a neologism, 'ma-mas' advocated the unity between malas and madigas. In his play *Ragavaashistham*, Bheemanna critiqued the brahminical interpretation of the origin and status of dalits rejecting their reading of certain Hindu classical texts. Far from being outcastes, Bheemanna held, dalits have a legitimate claim for higher social status and privilege.

Kusuma Dharmanna, a bitter critic of brahmins and Hinduism, launched a scathing attack in his famous speech:

> As Hinduism lacks in equality, Hindus in thousands, lakhs and crores converted to Isalm, Christianity, Buddhism, Jainism, Arya Samaj and Brahmo Samaj. It's Hindus who helped develop other religions. Every religion is set to expand itself. Everyone set one's eyes on us. They are eager to share us all through recruiting officers *a la* insurance agencies being seen everywhere. (Dharmanna 72)

He exposed the false, hypocritical and cunning nature of Hinduism. Treated as literary outcastes, Jashuva and other dalit writers of the period challenged the hegemonic attitude, and spearheaded self-respect movements independently of both the Congress and the Left.

Nationalist Literary Movement (1905-1945)

Put to both social and political use, the nationalist writers believed that the independence would herald a new birth of India. Several literary works came out on the theme of nationalism. Of them, Unnava Laxminarayana's *Malapalli* (1922) and N.G. Ranga's *Harijana Nayakudu* (1933) depict the untouchability and misery of dalits suggesting solutions within the caste system. Several other upper caste writers pursued in their works Gandhi's motto of 'harijan upliftment.'

Alongside the elite nationalist movement and writing, dalits ran a parallel nationalist movement, which did not find place in the literary and nationalist historiography. Dalits felt the need to set an agenda as different from the Gandhian movement, and produced dalit nationalist writing. Kusuma Dharmanna's famous song, *Makoddi Nalladorathanam* (we don't want this brown bureaucracy), written to counter the Gandhian writer, Garimilla Satyanarayana's song, "We Don't Want this European Bureaucracy," became instantly popular. Dharmanna believed that the independence would not liberate the dalits:

Fighting the government for self-rule,

they would ask for independence. But

they wouldn't give us independence,

they wouldn't allow us into temples and shrines,

they wouldn't allow us stay put in choultries.

they wouldn't allow us draw water from public wells.

They would say, malas have no rights. Oh god

if we have no rights,

what's the meaning of the Independence? (Dharmanna 23)

Another dalit nationalist poet, Jala Rangaswami critiqued the upper caste activities:

You prove that you are the

descendants of sages.

Outwardly you call us brothers

you boast to have listened to the teaching of Gandhi

nobody follows (him), it is not injustice

you forget the words of Mahatma Gandhi

*you burn with anger at the untouchables (*Rangaswamy 9*)*

The elite nationalist literature, having been failed to reflect the aspirations of the dalits, the latter wrote what may be termed the parallel nationalist works representing the dalit nationalism.

The nationalist writings, the brahmin-led progressive, revolutionary, feminist and Telangana writings, ignored caste and dalit writings deliberately and concertedly. The following analyses testify to this.

Progressive Literary Movement (1935-55)

Abhyudaya Rachayitala Sangham (ARASAM), progressive writers' association, founded in 1943, was a frontal organisation of the CPI, and the movement followed the waning bhava kavitvam (romantic poetry 1920-1935). Influenced by the socialist-communist ideology, the progressive writings began to be published as early as 1933. The incidents of the underground distribution of the ideological pamphlets, the publication of *Jwaala*, a periodical and the founding of the CPI led to the formation of ARASAM. The first conference was presided over by Tapi Dharma Rao at Tenali, the other progressive writers being Sri Sri, Narayana Babu, Pattabhi, Dasarathi, Kundurthi, Arudra, C. Narayana Reddy, among others. The paradox of ARASAM was that none of these progressive writers was an activist.

Fighting the imperialism and fascism, wedded to Marxist ideology, promoting the cause of the working class, ARASAM had no specific agenda for the annihilation of the caste. *Maha*

Prasthanam, (forward march) and *Maro Prapancham* (the other world) of Sri Sri, which are known for Sanskrit diction and Hindu imagery, far fetched from sudras/dalits, were used as symbols of change. The flaw of ARASAM was that it had been deliberately oblivious of the non-class aspects like caste, gender, ethnic group and religion, which existed in society. Indian Marxists, Dr Ambedkar observed, failed to understand and comprehend the caste-specific character of Indian Society. The ARASAM writers conveniently connived at the atrocities of the upper castes, social inequality and the question of dalits' self-respect.

The very titles of the anthologies/poems of the ARASAM writers—Niagara (1944), an anthology of progressive verse, Dasarathi's *Agnidhara* (1949) and *Rudraveena* (1950), Somasundar's *Vajrayudham* (1949), Arudra's *Tvamevaham* (1949), Anisetti's *Agniveena* (1949), Gangineni's *Vdayini* (1950), C. Vijayalakshmi's *Vishadabharatham* (1965), to name only a few—are indicative of the brahmins' preference for Sanskritised, elitist *marga* Telugu rather than *desi* tradition, which is closer to the language of the working classes, to use their own phrase. Disenchanted by its elitist character, the ARASAM writings began to wane by 1955. Some of the writers having abandoned ARASAM, the movement soon eclipsed as it is de-linked from people's language and social life.

Digambara Poetic Movement (1965-68)

The hopes of the independence that it would herald a new epoch having been shattered, coupled with price rise and unemployment, there was a widespread dissent among a cross section of people having its reverberations in literature. The complaisant mainstream writers were bombarded by six *Digambara Kavulu*, (naked poets), comprising Nagna Muni (M.H. Kesava Rao), Nikhileswar (Yadava Reddy), Jwala Mukhi (Veera Raghavacharyulu), Cherabanda Raju (Baddam Bhaskar Reddy), Bhairavayya (Man Mohan Sahay) and Maha Swapna (Kammisetti Venkateswara Rao). Startling the society with naked truths (hence the phrase naked poetry), they provided the much-needed jolt to Telugu literature by re-linking literature to society in their avant-garde kind of writing. Their concerns being poverty, unemployment and political indifference to the problems confronting the society, the naked poets made news about launching their anthologies: their first anthology was released in 1965 at a street-corner meeting by Nampalli Pandu, a rickshaw puller; the second in 1966 by Jangala Chitti, a hotel servant; the third, which had kick-started the modern Telugu literature, was dedicated in 1968 to Kanchikarla Kotesh, a dalit who was burnt alive by the upper castes accusing him of theft.

This incident could be considered the forerunner to the identity movements, of dalit, feminist and *adivasi*, in times to come. Their poetry is criticised to be hatred. Their influence being short lived, their protest criticised as anarchic, the Digambara poetry suffered from the limitation of not touching on the fundamental question of the caste. Having been failed to continue the tradition started by the dalit writers, the short lived movement ceased to be relevant as it lacked philosophical perspective and compelling world view.

Revolutionary Literary Movement (1970-80)

Viplava Rachayitala Sangham (VIRASAM), revolutionary writers' association, launched in 1970 is an avowed frontal organisation of the Maoist Party (erstwhile CPI (ML) Peoples War Group). It projected Sri Sri as its icon, the other prominent poets being Sivasagar, Gaddar, G. Kalyana Rao, Vara Vara Rao, Chenchaiah, K. Sivareddy, Vangapandu Prasada Rao, Cherabanda Raju, among others. Designated as *mahakavi*, great poet, Sri Sri claimed that the literary century 'belonged to him' meaning he wielded influence on literature for a century. Known for progressive and surrealistic elements, he is said to have pioneered and gave a new look to modern Telugu poetry. A master of poetic diction, Sri Sri is acknowledged as 'a splendid alchemist.' The dalit critics however consider him brahminical because of his excessive obsession with Sanskrit diction and Hindu imagery.

The immediate impetus to VIRASAM was the Srikakulam Peasant Uprising (1967) led by Vempatapu Satyanarayana and Adibatla Kailasam with a slogan, 'land to the tiller.' In literature, Subbarao Panigrahi was declared as its source of inspiration. Varavara Rao, one of its founder members, continues to be on its executive committee ever since its inception. The peasant struggles for land however did not benefit the dalits, who were not tenants or tillers; only labourers.

Ever since the launch of VIRASAM, it has essentially been exclusivist regarding the dalit question. Frustrated by this, Sivasagar, a prominent revolutionary dalit poet, and the founder member of the then People' War (ML), resigned to his membership of the Central Committee and walked out of the Party in 1985 coinciding with the Karamchedu massacre, accusing the leadership of being casteist in its policies and organisational structure. Sivasagar's departure from VIRASAM triggered a shift in dalit writers from class to caste. Ever since, dalit poets, (dalits constitute the *dalams*, cadre, the upper castes being at the helm of affairs) criticised the Party on the grounds that the working class struggles do not serve the dalit cause; that the land struggles did not benefit the dalits; that VIRASAM neglected dalit writings. Following Sivasagar, several other young poets like Vemula Yellaiah, Koyi Koteswar Rao, J. Goutam critiqued in their poetry both the moderate and the extreme left. Goutam writes in his poem, "Beware of Maoism":

Hello, comrades, red salutes to you!

If you come to know about the farmers' suicides

tell them that

the Russian disintegration was abetted by America

the investments in China are firming up the Revolution!

Explain the sudras and chandalas

that Manudharma is better than the Constitution, and

that Bhimrao is a liberal bourgeois

In the light of the identity movements taking place in different parts of the country, VIRASAM in its state conference announced a paradigm shift from *only* the class to caste, gender, minority, tribals and regional identity movements considering that the experience of the subjects needs to be taken into account, and that the personal experiences of the subordinated people are outcome of particular social constructions. However, the stance of VIRASAM has been criticised by its staunch critics like B.S. Ramulu, who held that only those subjects having the experience of the subjugated self are legitimately competent to talk about their experiences of marginality and struggles.

Feminist Literary Movement (1980-2000)

One of the main contentions of the dalit women has been regarding the silence of the elite feminists on the issue of caste as a gendering agency. The first ever anthology of women writing, *Manaku Teliyani Manacharitra*, 1986 (*We were Making History*), life stories of women in the Telangana People's Struggle; Tripuraneni Srinivas' *Gurichoosi Pade Paata* (singing with aimed target); 1990 and *Neelimeghalu* (blue clouds) 1993, edited by Volga do not represent the dalit writers adequately. A recent anthology, *Mudra: Vanithala Kavithalu* (2001) edited by Subhadra Devi and Bhargavi Rao compiling a hundred poems by women covering from the fifteenth century to the present also neglected dalit representation.

The anthologies, associations and media debates of the elite feminists point to two important trends: that their concern is primarily the family, de-mystification of motherhood, violence and sexuality; and that they neglected dalit women's writings. *Neelimeghalu,* which carried only a dalit and a Muslim minority poet among thirty and odd poets (amounting to mere three poems out of a total of ninety), generated considerable amount of debate on the question of framing the gendering. Most of the poems explicitly deal with family, body and sexuality. In a different context, however, women's body and sexuality was described in what is known as *sringara*, sensuous writing by men. When women chose to write, it attracted criticism. SV Rama Rao, for example, criticised feminist poetry on the grounds that the anthology does not represent "all the women; it reflects only the desires of the urban, bigheaded rich young girls. It does not represent the economic, social and political exploitation." He further attacked the poetry as the one "dealing with urine, menses, bleeding" (213). The mainstream feminism has sought to challenge "the family, the authority-based relationships between men and women and the patriarchal structure that hides the male dominance which attributes holiness to motherhood" (Shyamala, 15). Dalit writers and activists challenge through their praxis of activism and writings.

The elite feminists have been silent on the casteist male attacks on dalit women. The Karamchedu struggle exposed the hypocrisy of the elite feminists. Representing themselves, the dalit women fought in the Karamchedu struggle with militancy. They stood in the forefront of the struggle. The Karamchedu, Tsunduru, Vempenta and other atrocities "bore out the fact that women's sexuality is the key link to maintaining the hierarchical structures of caste." (Mohanty 242)

Dalit women's writing, contrarily, mark a shift from the concerns of the elite feminists. Instead of family, de-mystification of motherhood and sexuality, the dalit women focus on caste-based patriarchy. The shift is from family and body to the caste-based patriarchy: "There have been very few dalit poems that discuss the theme of the family...the preoccupation with family is more of an upper-caste, middle-class phenomenon that does not affect most dalit women, who belong to lower classes and castes" (Sridahr 239). Dalit women's writing marks a departure from the elite feminists in regard to family and women.

The elite feminists in Andhra Pradesh formed a social forum, besides several others earlier, by name *Manalo Manam* (among ourselves) as a broad forum apparently encompassing the women from a cross section of women, including the dalits. As a symbolic gesture, a dalit has been incorporated into its executive. But the forum and its agenda has quickly become the subject of criticism by the dalit women on the grounds that it has no agenda for the liberation of dalit women; the forum is silent on the question of the oppression of dalit women by the upper caste women. This led to the floating of a parallel forum, *Maalo Memu* (we are ourselves). The dalit women activists and writers have been actively engaged in framing the issues concerning dalit women as essentially different from those of the elite women both in the debates and literary anthologies.

Dalit women brought out an anthology, *Nallapoddu* (dark sunrise) in 2004 tracing the tradition of dalit women writing as far back as 1921. This anthology could be considered a dalit response to *Neelimeghalu*, an anthology by elite feminists. Considering that *Nallapoddu* suffered from limitations that it represents mala as well as coastal writers, another anthology, *Nallaregati Saallu* (furrows of black soil), stories on madiga and its sub-castes, was published in 2006. The dalit women intelligentsia in the last decade contributed to the emergence of dalit feminism offering sharp critique of the exclusivist, elite feminism. Jupaka Subhadra, Gogu Shyamala, Jajula Gowri, M.M. Vinodini, Challapalli Swarupa Rani, Sujatha Gidla, among others, have produced a considerable body of writing. Besides the literary genres like short story, poetry and personal/family narratives, a great deal of media-based debate on feminism has been taking place. The dalit writing and debates by women is sharp and more focused than the writings of their men counterparts: "the poetry by dalit women writing [sic] from the dalit women's perspective and based on their experiences as dalit women is far more powerful and has a far greater impact than the poetry of dalit male poets or upper caste women poets. Dalit women's issues have less in common with dalit men's issues than with those of the upper caste women (Swaroopa Rani 21). The dalit women's writing, thus, represents the concerns that are unique to themselves.

Revival of Dalit Movement (1985-)

The revival of modern dalit period is marked by atrocities against the Dalits. The Karamchedu massacre in 1981, Tsunduru in 1991 triggered the otherwise complaisant dalit writing and movement. Kathi Padma Rao and Bojja Tarakam organised the dalits under an organisation, Dalita Mahasabha in 1985, which waged relentless fight for justice. Karamchedu created a rupture in communist discourse too. A new group of dalit writers having emerged, popular dalit balladeers and performers from the ranks of the communist movement took to dalit stance. They include Nassar, a burrakatha performer, Suddala Hanumanthu, a song composer and singer and the legendary balladeer Gaddar.

Karamchedu broke the silence on the part of the dalits, who were with the left. Gaddar's most popular song "Dalit Pululamma" became instantly popular in the dalit struggles. The post-Karamchedu and Tsunduru phase produced notable dalit leaders, orators, writers and balladeers. The awareness brought about by the organised dalit movement subsequently branched out into the identity struggles. Culminating in the Dandora movement, the sub-caste writing and the dalit gender began to construct the dalit liberation theory.

Telangana Literary Movement

Being under the reign of the Kakatiya Dynasty from 1000 to 1323; the Kutubshahi and Asafjahi dynasties from 1720 to 1948; having been made a part of the Indian Union after the famous Police Action, 1948; waging a peasants' armed struggle (1946-51); forcibly merged with Andhra region in 1956 against the wishes of its people, the Telangana has been subjected to both external and internal colonisation after the Kakatiya reign. During the reigns after Kakatiya, the people of the Telangana have had unique experience different from those of their counter parts in the other regions of the state. With a unique cultural history and identity, the Telangana region produced its writings presenting a picture of its rich cultural heritage and a desolate picture with rampant poverty, illiteracy, child labour, farmer suicides, unemployment, and water and electricity shortages—all due to discrimination. In the struggles, movements and agitations of different hues, sudras and dalits played a prominent role. Their voices stifled, their roles being obliterated in the literary, social and political historiography of Telangana, the regional identity and the history of the cultural subjugation have been extensively written about, especially by sudras and dalits.

A lot of debate about the Telangana literature has been generated over the years in opposition to Andhra writings focusing on regional experience, language and the primacy accorded to the writers. Concerning language, the Telangana protagonists questioned the legitimacy of standard or acceptable variety of language. When Telangana dialect is promoted, the dialect as employed by Kundurti Anjaneyulu, Kaloji Narayana Rao and Dasarathi-brothers is projected as the Telangana dialect: they employ rural karanam/brahmin variety, which is distinct from the register largely spoken by the rural sudras and dalits. The latter have not been accorded due importance in the genre of the Telangana literature. For example, the Telangana literary historiography makes no reference to *Jamba Puranam*, a unique art form performed by the Telangana dakkalis. It is a different matter that a version of it has recently been published in 2011. Similarly, Dunna Iddasu, the first madiga writer from the Telangana region finds no mention in the history of literature.

The Telangana activist-dalit writers like Manda Krishna Madiga, Vemula Yellaiah, Jupaka Subhadra, Gogu Shyamala, Krupakar Madiga and several others floated the idea of what they termed the 'social Telangana' arguing that the formation of the geographical Telangana would fail the dalits of the region. It does not escape the notice of the Telanganan protagonists that the dalits are in the forefront in spearheading the movement. The balladeers like Gorati Venkanna, Gaddar, Andhesri, Rasamai Balakishan, Vimalkka and scores of the others have become trend setters in molding public opinion and taking the message to the masses through the song. In the mass agitations for separate Telangana, the song and the ballet have become integral to the movement, and the performers are invariably dalits. The writers, columnists, academics and the cadre of the parties involved in the movement for the separate Telangana too are mostly dalits, who are determined to have their say in matters of activism, theory and literary writings.

References

Bharathi, Vijaya, B. *Puranalu Kula Vyavastha*, Hyderabad: Hyderabad Book Trust, 2001. Print.

Dharmanna, Kusuma. *Makoddi Nalladoratanamu.* Hyderabad: HBT, 2003. Print.

——. "Samyavadanni Sahinchani Hinduism," *Nalupu.* 1992. Print.

Ilaiah, Kancha. *Utpathi-Telugu Sahitya Varasatvam.* Hyderabad: HBT, 2003. Print.

Lalita, K. *Manaku Teliyani Mana Charitra*. Hyderabad: Stree Shakti Sangatana, 1986. Print.

Mohanty, Manoranjan. *Caste, Class and Gender.* New Delhi: Sage Publications, 2004. Print.

Narayana Rao, Velcheru. "Coconut and Honey: Sanskrit and Telugu in Medieval Andhra." *Social Scientist.* Vol. 23 Nos. 10-12, (October-December, 1995). Print.

Ramakrishna, V. "Literary and Theater movements in Colonial Andhra: Struggle for Left Ideological Legitimacy." *Social Scientist.* Vol. 21, Nos. 1-2, 1993. Print.

Rama Rao, S.V. in *Neelimeghalu*. Hyderabad: Swetcha Prachuranalu, 1993. Print.

Rangaswami, Jala, cited in Satyanarayana, A. *Dalits and Uppercastes: Essays in Social History*. New Delhi: Kanishka Publishers, 2005. Print.

Satyanarayana, A. *Dalits and Upper Castes.* New Delhi: Kanishka Publishers, 2005. Print.

Swaroopa Rani, Challapalli. "Dalit Women's Writing in Telugu." *Economic and Political Weekly*. April 25, 1998. Print.

Sridhar, M. and Uma, Alladi. "The Self and the Family in Telugu Women's Poetry," ed Dasgupta, Sanjukta and Malasri Lal, *Indian family in transition: Literary and Cultural Texts.* New Delhi: Sage, 2997. Print.

Shyamala, Gogu. *Nallapoddu: Dalita Streela Sahityam 1921–2002*. Hyderabad: HBT, 2006. Print.

3

The Rise of Telugu Dalit Novel

Telugu novel as a genre emerged after the colonial reform of the language especially by C.P. Brown (1798-1884) and the required impetus of the nationalist movement. The other modernist movements—progressive, revolutionary and feminist—made the novel focused and topical moving away from the banal themes of the metaphysical, mysticism and love. Several liberal writers chose dalits as the protagonists as well as the themes. However, the pre-independence social novel, the post-independence political novel and the movement novel in the modern period failed to represent the life, contradictions and liberation of the dalits. The upper caste novels on the dalits suffer from certain limitations as their corresponding movements did. The emergence of the dalit novel, shaped by the identity movements, is both a challenge and reply to the limitations of the upper caste novelists. The dalit novel and short fiction by the dalits is more affirmative of the dalitness compared to poetry. This article critiques the portrayal of the dalits in the upper caste novel; and maps the emergence of the dalit novel as a genre.

Language Reform

The emergence of the Indian novel in the nineteenth century was made possible by the reform and the modernisation of the Indian languages by the English bureaucrat turned linguists. Necessitated by the British-Indian administration, the English officers had learnt the Indian languages to understand and serve the people better. Not stopping with proficiency, they mastered the languages, evolved the grammars and served the languages and literatures. Notable among them were C.P. Brown, Charles Wilkins, A.D. Campbell, who reformed Telugu; William Jones, Sanskrit; Benjamin, Malayalam; William Carey, Marathi, Sanskrit, Punjabi, Telugu; Schultz, Gordon, Pritchett, among others.

Guided by the 'principle of economy,' approximation of the spoken to the written form and the learner friendly approach, the reformers dropped and changed some letters of alphabet, which used to be queer and farfetched from the spoken mode. They simplified the complex orthography making the languages printing-enabled and accessible to the commoners. With the simplification and modernisation of the languages, the prose began to be used for writing to communicate. The influence of the English novel coupled with writer and learner-friendly changes, Indians began to write novels. Meenakshi Mukherjee writes, "English education and through English as exposure to Western literature influenced the birth of Indian novel" (Mukherjee 3). The English officers encouraged the lettered brahmins to write novels about the Telugu life.

Social Novel

The first novel in Telugu, *Rangaraja Cheritramu* (1872) was written by Naraharisetti Gopalakrishna, a government servant in Kurnool, as a nomination to a competition. The elite hero in the novel Srirangaraju falls in love with Sonabai, a lambadi (tribal) woman. The novel ends happily when her identity of being a princess was revealed. Given the social hierarchy of the late nineteenth century, the novel could be considered a step in modernity so far as the portrayal of a tribal character is concerned. The writer's choice of a lambadi woman as a character and the positive portrayal may be understood as a necessity to sound progressive so as to impress upon the English officers, especially since the novel was written for the competition.

The next novel in the lineage was Kandukuri Veereshalingam's (1948-1919) *Rajashakara Charitram* (1878), a social novel, considered the first in Telugu. Known as the founder of modern Telugu literature, Kandukuri originally set out to translate Oliver Goldsmith's *The Vicar of Wakefield,* but later changed his mind to write a novel instead of translation. The novel is critical of superstitions, and adopted a rational approach to life: "Kandukuri regarded social justice and reform more urgent than political liberation" (Vijayasree 112). The focus is on the individual reform with the backdrop of the decaying feudalism. The novel depicts the life of the middle-class brahmins during the late nineteenth century.

Other novels of this genre include T. Suryanarayana's *Helavathi* (1913), which is reflective of the sympathy of the humanitarian upper castes, who were interested in the upliftment of the dalits. The novel reflects the "contradictions of the middle classes, upper caste writers and readers...in respect of their attitude towards the caste system (Das 305). Venkata Parvatiswara Kavulu's *Matrmandiram* (1919) on the dalits' entry into the temple; and Veluri Shivarama Sastri's *Obaiah* (1920) are the other novels of interest.

Nationalist/Political Novel

The construction of nationalism was necessitated by two factors: to counter the large scale conversions of the Hindus to Christianity; and to counter and connive at the growing dalit movements being waged—both of which were seen as the threats to Hinduism. Exposed to and influenced by the European liberalism, the educated Indians preferred to be drawn by the nationalist struggle conveniently ignoring the more demanding and urgent problem of caste and retrogressive ethos of the social elites.

Jnanpith laureate, Viswanatha Satyanarayana's (1895-1976) *Veyipadagalu* (thousand hoods) (1921), translated into Hindi as *Sahasraphan* by P.V. Narasimha Rao, portrays three generations of the Telugu people. Using a half-man, half-snake character by name Pasirika (pasture), the novelist deals with corruption, this according to him is a result of materialism. Anti-British, anti-Industrialisation, anti-modern, the novel reaffirms the traditional belief and polygamy. The novelist approves of an upper caste man marrying a woman from each of the lower castes. Being revivalist, the novel suggests the dharma and the Hindu family as panacea to the ethical, moral, economic, social and cultural crises. With its revivalist stance and the affirmation of family and the Hindu dharma, the novel is avowedly anti-dalit without qualms.

Another anti-dalit novel written the following year, but this time around disguisedly, is Unnava Laxminarayana's most acclaimed work *Malapalli* (Malas' hamlet) (1922). The novel is representative of the unity of the upper castes in neglecting a demanding problem. Gandhi considered it "one of the best novels that supported the nationalist movement" (in Enoch 90).

Noted dalit academic, critic and writer, Prof Kolakaluri Enoch considers *Malapalli* a novel supportive of the upper castes in the guise of supporting the dalits. The novel was written against the backdrop of the Justice Party, launched in 1917 as a part of the anti-brahmin movement in the Madras Presidency. Led by T.M. Nayar and Theagoraya Chetty, the movement demanded jobs for the non-brahmins, Christians and Muslims as against the practice of offering the jobs only to the brahmins, who had preferred English education and became the first bilinguals in the country to grab all the jobs. Guided by the belief that they were exploited by both the English and brahmins, the movement got transformed into the self-respect movement led by Periyar E.V. Ramaswamy in the subsequent period.

Unnava, having opposed the Justice Party, had to serve a sentence in the jail, during which he wrote *Malapalli*. Intended to be propaganda for nationalism, the novelist projects those dalits, who opposed the Justice Party. Apparently seeming to be supportive of the dalits, the novelist actually supports the dalits, who were with the Congress and were Vaishnavites. The novel opposes religious conversions and is critical of the Saivites as well as the Justice Party. Acclaimed equally by communists and Congress, the novel became much more popular especially when it was banned by the Madras Presidency. The novel became an all-time classic primarily due to the clever manipulation of the dalits as the theme, persona and language. Contrarily Enoch views: "the novel is anti-dalit and anti-Justice party" (Enoch 91). The novel glorifies *Ramarajya*, the Gandhian version of the welfare state and the Hindu nationalism concertedly opposing the concept of multiple identities.

N.G. Ranga's (1900-1995) *Harijana Nayakudu* (harijan leader) (1933), written under the influence of Unnava's *Malapalli*, focuses on the need for peasant-worker coalition for harmony between peasants and labourers. The story deals with a dalit agricultural labourer, who attempts a social reformation of his community, and succeeds, in his attempt with the help of his landlord's son. The novel concludes on a note that the happiness of the labourers lies in the peasants being at the helm of affairs, and the labourers being at the receiving end. A conversation between the dalit leader and the peasant testifies to this:

'I along with my community will always serve the peasants with loyalty, patience and strength, for the generosity you have showered upon me.'

Ramanayya, the kamma landlord blesses Basavalingayya, 'like you, the entire community of yours should serve us faithfully, loyally and with respect' (85).

Ranga makes the dalit agricultural labourers praise the benevolence of the rich peasant class. Belonging to kamma caste, Oxford educated, and having begun his activism as a Marxist, N.G. Ranga emerged as an important peasant leader pursuing the interests of the landed peasants in the delta region.

Yet another novel in dalit disguise is Muppala Ranganayakamma's (b.1939) *Balipeetham* (pedestal of sacrifice) (1953) which, apparently seems to be supportive of dalits, but in fact denigrates the dalit identity and self-respect. Bhaskar, a dalit marries Aruna, an upper caste ailing woman, who desired to die as a *sumangali*, a married woman. After his magnanimous gesture of marrying her, Aruna survives. Realising the enormity of the consequences, Aruna finds it difficult to live in a dalit's house because of their language, dressing and food habits. Inter-caste marriage between a dalit man and a brahmin woman as the focus of the novel, the handling of the theme discourages the practice of an upper caste woman marrying a dalit man. Frustrated, Aruna goes back to her aunt and uncle. She fails to understand the noble gesture of her dalit husband, who is interested in her health in contrast to her relatives, who are more interested in her wealth. Though regrets of her misdeeds to her dalit husband, Aruna understands from her cousin Kamala, who is happily married to a Christian, that marrying a Christian is better than marrying a dalit. An avowed Marxist and feminist, Ranganayakamma attempts to glorify the practice of the inter-caste marriages, but in the process, portrays the dalits and their culture as impertinent.

Palagummi Padmaraju's (1915-83) *Ramarajyaniki Rahadari* (pathway to welfare state) (1972) is a critique of the followers of the Gandhian notion of nationalism. Published in the modern period, the novel examines the Gandhian thought in retrospect by demystifying the aura of Gandhi and nationalism. The novelist portrays the Justice Party and its leadership belonging to Nayudus (kamma caste) in an antithetical manner. The polemics between brahmin and the non-brahmin upper caste leadership is interesting, when the latter adopts the stance of pro-British as a part of power sharing:

> We are patriots too. We too claim that India should be ruled by Indians. But who are Indians? At the present moment Brahmins dominate Indian society. They have suppressed the other communities for centuries. They kept the other castes in ignorance. Congress in the south India is led by brahmins. We do not consent the power to be transferred to the brahmins. (Padmaraju 142)

By portraying the characters antithetical to each other, the novelist vindicates that the rule of British India was better. To an uninformed reader, the novelist's position may sound very progressive in being anti-brahminical. In seeming to be critical of the brahmin leadership, and in projecting an alternative leadership, the novelist ignores two predominant issues: the parallel nationalist movement led by the dalits and projecting dalits as a part of the alternative leadership. Criticising the brahmin-led nationalist movement in the heyday of the revolutionary literary movement (1970-80) might sound progressive, but projecting an alternative leadership in Naidus, the other upper caste, oblivious of the dalit leadership, needs to be construed as retrogressive and anti-dalit.

Rachakonda Viswanathasastry's *Govulostunnayi Jagratha* (Beware, the cows are coming) (1973) is about the elite Indians who became Congressmen at the time of transfer of power. Rajabhogi, a British supporter, kidnaps Lachayamma, a beautiful woman of cow herders, and threatens her family with killing. Rajabhogi, who becomes a Congressman to escape punishment, becomes Rajayogi, with Lachayamma imprisoned in his palace. When the people revolt, Lachayamma's cow, symbolic of her son, kills Rajayogi. The novel is critical of non-violence, which is used as a mask for elites. The writer is an avowed leftist, and the most acclaimed of the modernists because of his deft use of prose and technique. But his world view completely misses the dalits.

Similarly, Mahidara Rammhana Rao's *Kollayi Kattitenemi* and Kesavareddy's *Incredible Goddess*, among other works, suffer from limitations in representing the dalits.

The Hyderabad state ruled by Nizam, having a different socio-political history from the rest of the colonial Andhra, produced political novel of protest. The Telangana people, having been reeled under poverty, atrocities of local landlords and *razakars*, militia of the MIM, the novel is tinged with the element of protest. The novels had the Telangana liberation movement as its backdrop. With an upsurge of the armed struggle turning violent, thousands of villages were liberated from the landlords and lacks of acres of land was distributed among the peasantry by the Communist Party of India (CPI). Deplorably, the lands however were given back to the landlords after the unification of the Hyderabad state with the Indian union. There is a strong criticism about the peasants' armed struggle and its outcome. While the communists claim that land had been distributed among the peasants, the dalits contrarily accuse that far from getting lands, several dalits, who formed the cadre of the armed struggle, lost their lives.

The armed struggle followed the famous police action by the union government liberating Telangana on Sept 17, 1948. The activists who had taken part in the struggle includes writers like Makdoom, the Dasaradhi brothers, Kaloji Narayana Rao, Vattikota Alwaruswamy, Sudhala Hanmanthu and Thirunagari Ramanjaneyulu. The social background of the writers being brahmins, and the guiding spirit of the struggles being Marxism, the political novel of the armed struggle neglected the dalit question. Except using the dalits as the protagonists in some of the novels, the dalits and their identity is not portrayed properly.

Vattikota Alwaruswamy's *Prajala Manishi* (people's man) (1952) and *Gangu* (1965) portray life in the Hyderabad state with a focus on the atrocities of the Nizam's rule and the exploitation of the local landlords and the militant struggle of the people against the Nizam as well as the landlords. Dasaradhi Rangacharya's (b.1928) *Chillaradevullu* (The Lesser Deities) (1969) written in the Telangana dialect, portrays the pathetic condition of the poor, who are exploited by the Reddy landlords. Gollapudi Narayana Rao's *Telugu Gadda* (Telugu land) (1968) and Maheedhara Rammohun Rao's *Kollayi Gattitenemi* represent the life in Telangana.

Dalit Novel

Beginning from 1960, dalits began to write themselves. Enoch who may be considered the forerunner of the dalit novel in Telugu published *Samata* (1960) and *Anaadha* (1961). Only after 1980, the novels with dalit consciousness began to appear. Boya Jangaiah's *Jatara* (1988), G Rama Mohan Rao's (Spartacus) *Kakibathukulu*, (Police lives, 1991), Chilukuri Devaputra's *Panchamam* (1998), P. Nasaraiah's *Madigapalle* (1998), G. Kalyana Rao's *Antarani Vasantam* (Untouchable Spring) (2000),

Vemula Yellaiah's *Kakka* (2000) and *Siddi* (2006), Gopararu Nageshwar Rao's *Dandemmeedi Chilukalu* (2001) and *Maromaarpu* (2002) deal with the dalit experience and contradictions.

In Chilukuri Devaputra's *Panchamam*, Shivaiah the protagonist is a madiga, who pursues higher education with the encouragement of an upper caste man. Shivaiah becomes an officer, and the upper castes, who become ministers, do not want the land reforms implemented in their region. When Sivaiah refuses to oblige them, the landlords get him suspended on charge of bribe. The deputy chief minister, being a madiga, too is helpless in protecting Shivaiah. The novelist drives home the point that the existing constitutional institutions cannot change the lives of the dalits.

Mohan Rao's *Kaki Bathukulu* revolves around the story of his father, a constable. Prakasam, the protagonist begins to find out that casteism exists in the police force. Poorly paid, ill-treated, being unpaid servants at police officers' homes, the dalit constables are the most exploited. Prakasam struggles hard to maintain his honesty and self-respect. Written in 804 pages, the novel encompasses the period from early 1940s to 1975 covering many incidents that include the freedom movement and the armed struggle. Having been served a show cause notice for writing about the police department, the author ascertained his right to write just as the upper caste police officers wrote earlier. Mohan Rao exposes the rigidity of the police department generating a debate.

Antaraani Vasantham, translated into English as *Untouchable Spring* is the most acclaimed dalit novel in Telugu dealing with six generations of people and their socio-cultural life, humiliations and oppression by the forward castes. The main thrust of the novel begins and ends with the birth and the death of Yellaiah, the grandfather of Ruth's husband, Ruben. Yellaiah experiences in his childhood both physical and mental trauma on account of untouchability. Chased by the caste-Hindus, Yellaiah runs into a dalit artist and masters the art from him. By the fag end of his life, he would return to his village, Enneladinni, during the famine, and dies on joining his wife and his grown up son. The first half of the novel, dealing with agrarian relations, the atrocities, the caste relations in the village, transition of the villages–all of which subject the malas and the madigas to abject poverty, insults and repression.

In the second half of the novel, there is a shift in the thrust of the novel from the caste-struggle to the class-struggle. Yellaiah's grandchildren, Ruth and Ruben and great grandchildren, Mary Suvartha, Emmanuel, Jessy and Ruby work as cadre in the underground Left. Ruben would ruminate, like Gorky's Mother, the struggle and sacrifice of her progeny, and derives fulfillment out of it. The second half of the novel carries out polemics of class struggles, glorifying sacrifice, bloodshed, vibrancy and the volatility of the dalit life reminding one of *Vasantha Geetham*, a novel of anonymous authorship. Kalyana Rao's portrayal of the dalit life is guided by his ideology of Marxism and Leninism. In terms of history, the class-based militant struggles may be realistic in parts of Andhra Pradesh. But there is the other side of it too. Most of the people who lost their lives in the name of militant struggles were the dalits, whose children are deprived of parents; wives deprived of husbands.

Vemula Yellaiah's eponymous novel, *Kakka* deals with madigas portraying dalit experience in terms of poverty, disputes and violence. Having resolved the problem of his widowed mother by getting her suitably remarried, Kakka begins his life as a child-farmhand. Kakka and his mother Kalemma are not considered a part of the madigas, and the fellow madigas refuse to allow them into the community. The *rachabanda*, pedestal of justice stands as a symbol of injustice. Kakka is denied of justice from his caste men and also from the the government. Ending inconclusively, the novel portrays the socio-political scenario of the Telangana region dealing with the conspiracy of Visalandhra and the atrocities of Reddy and Kamma landlords.

The novel is known for deviation from the mainstream as well as the dalit writing in respect of the style and the language. His effort is to reclaim, to privilege, to centre the dalit language. He uses the Telangana dialect both in the dialogue and narrative. For the first time, the novel is written in the madiga register in the oral form. This is in keeping with the illiteracy of the dalit characters and situations in the novel. His experiments with the Telangana dialect, madiga register and oral mode are aimed at legitimising the dalitness of language. *Kakka* is thus a deviation even from the contemporary Telugu dalit literature.

Conclusion

Dalit novel in Telugu by the upper castes cannot be termed progressive or liberal, let alone dalit. The fact that the dalits were written about by the upper castes in itself does not qualify it to belong to the genre of dalit novel. In comparative terms, for instance, with Indian novel in English, the upper castes had no qualms in using the names of castes and having dalits as protagonists in their novels. Indian novel in English, in its search for secular and modern, turned out to be hypocritical in the avoidance of caste references overtly or covertly. The Indian English novelists took care of choosing the names of the protagonists without the nuances of the caste. Makarand Paranjape, in his survey of the Indian English novel observes that the English novelists and their protagonists are invariably brahmins, which is not true of the novel in Telugu and other regional languages. The emergence of the dalit novel in Telugu has undoubtedly radicalised the contemporary writing in Telugu in that the latter is growing to be focused, progressive and inclusive. This may be termed the signal achievement of and contribution to the Telugu writing.

References

Alwaruswamy, Vattikota. *Prajala Manishi.* Hyderabad: Vishalandhra Publishers, 1955. Print.

Arudra. *Samagrandhra Sahityam.* Vol. 12, Vijayawada: Prajashakti Book House, 1991. Print.

Campbell, A.D. *A Grammar of the Telugu Language.* Madras: Government Press, 1816. Print.

Das, Sisir Kumar. *A History of Indian Literature 1911-1956 Struggle for Freedom: Triumph and Tragedy.* New Delhi: Sahitya Academy, 2996. Print.

Enoch, Kolakaluri. "Telugulo Dalita ahityam," *Sahitya Sandarshanm: Parishodhana Patraprasangalu.*Anantha-puram: Jyoti Grandhamala, 2005. Print.

Gopalakrishna, Naraharisetti. *Sri Rangarayacharitra.* Madras: Vyavahara Tarangini Press, 1872. Print.

Kalyana Rao, G. *Untouchable Spring*, trans. Alladi Uma and Sreedhar. New Delhi: Orient-Blackswan, 2010. Telugu original was published in 2000. Print.

Mukherjee, Meenakhsi. *Realism and Reality: the Novel and Society in India.* New Delhi: OUP, 1985. Print.

Narayana Rao, Velcheru. "Political Novel in Telugu." Ed E. J. Brill-Leiden, *Contributions to Asian Studies,* Vol. VI, Canadian Association for South Asian Studies, 1975. Print.

Padmaraju, Palagummi. *Ramarajyaniki Rahadari.* Vijayawada: Emesco Pocket Books, 1972. Print.

Paranjape, Makarand. "Caste of Indian English Novel." *Economic and Political Weekly.* (Oct 5, 1991). Print.

Prabhakar Rao, S.S. "Telugu." *The Growth of the Novel in India.* Ed P.K. Rajan, New Delhi: Abhinav Publications, 1989. Print.

Ramamohana Rao. *Kollayi Gattitenemi.* Vijayawada: Navya Rachana Mandali, 1965. Print.

Rangacharya Dasarathi. *The Lesser Deities,* trans. Chakravathi

Seshacharya, Hyderabad: PS Telugu University, 1997. Print.

Satyanarayana, K. "Politics of (Self)-Representation: Case of a 'De-Brahminised' Brahmin." *EPW* (Nov 23, 1991). Print.

Subbarayudu, G.K. and Vijayasree. "Twentieth Century Telugu Literature." *Handbook of Twentieth Century Literatures of India*. Print.

Tabish Khair, *Babu Fictions: Alienation in Contemporary Indian English novels*. New Delhi: OUP, 2001. Print.

Thirumali. "Dora and Gadi: Manifestation of Landlord Domination in Telangana." *Economic and Political Weekly*. Vol. 27: No. 9, (Feb 29, 1992). Print.

Veerabhadrarao, Kothapalli. *Telugu Sahityampai English Prabhavam*. Secunderabad: Sivaji Press, 1960. Print.

Vijayasree, C. "The Birth of a Genre: Telugu Novel in the Nineteenth Century." Ed Meenakshi Mukherjee, *Early Novels in India*, New Delhi: Sahitya Academy, 2002. Print.

Viswanatha Sastri, Rachakonda. *Beware, the Cows are Coming*, trans. Alladi Uma and Sreedhar. New Delhi: Sahitya Academy, 2001. Print.

Yellaiah, Vemula. *Kakka*, Nalgonda: Gosangi, 2000. Print.

4

Reclaiming Madiga Identity: Vemula Yellaiah's *Kakka*

Vemula Yellaiah's *Kakka* (2000), a madiga dalit novel, depicts the madiga life in the post-independence Telangana. The agrarian relations, madiga culture and ritual, politics of anti-Nizam agitation, inter-caste rivalries, hostility against the dalits and the futility of the State in changing the dalits' lives are some of the aspects portrayed so realistically that they sound stranger than fiction to those who are not familiar with the rural dalit life. The novel deals with the lives of three generations: Kakka, his mother and grandmother. Kakka and his mother suffer on account of the external as well as the internal contradictions of the caste. His problems as a madiga are compounded by the contradictions within the madiga community. The novelist privileges with pride, in keeping with the madigas' self-respect and identity movements, the madiganess that was earlier a matter of shame, insult and recoil. This article considers *Kakka* as an attempt at reclaiming madiga identity.

Madiga Patriarchy

An inward looking dalit novel, *Kakka* portrays dalit experience in terms of poverty, disputes and violence. The dalit life in the pre-independence period was led by slavery and gleaning the leftovers as represented by the grandmother.

The second generation dalit life is portrayed through Kakka's mother, Kalemma, a widow. Her own caste men subject her to physical and mental violence accusing her of sexual relations; alienate her and her son from the madiga caste. Meting out inhuman torture, the mother and the son are excommunicated denying them work. Her son, Kakka resolves her problem by getting her suitably remarried. Widow remarriages have been common among dalits and sudras. Kakka meanwhile grows into a mature adult realising that the problem of caste is too complicated subjecting the dalits to oppression both within and outside the caste.

The novel begins with his grandmother's recounting of the travails she had faced, especially the way her son (Kakka's father) died of a scorpion-bite while tilling the wet-fields of the Reddy landlords. Then on, Kakka begins his life as a child farmhand. His problems begin with the death of Ayyamma, his grandmother. Kakka and his mother Kalemma are left to themselves as they are not considered a part of the madigas. The fellow madigas refuse to allow them into the community. They are alienated within the madiga community.

Kakka, the child, who works as a contract labourer, is persecuted by the landlords. Therefore, his mother decides to stop him from work by squaring off the debt against which Kakka works. When she proposes to sell her share of whatever little land she owned, her brother-in-law, who too claims a stake, refuses to cooperate with her in selling the land. On the contrary, he attempts to seduce her taking advantage of her loneliness. When she refuses to submit herself to him, he conspires to take revenge against her by sending her out of the village. As a part of his ploy, he alleges that she has an illicit relationship with a neighbouring farmhand, who used to frequent her for discussing her child's persecution by the landlords.

Rachabanda: Symbol of Injustice

Justice is not delivered to women and dalits in the traditional settlements of disputes in villages. The novelist uses *rachabanda*, the open place for settlement of disputes, as a symbol of injustice.

Rachabanda is used in two contexts. The dispute of alleged extramarital relationship is brought to the *rachabanda* by a man. The headmen of the caste mete out inhuman punishment to Kalemma. The punishment includes battering her, dipping her fingers in simmering oil, making her hold a heated crowbar and so on. The caste men hang a garland of worn-out sandals on her house, raise a fence of thorny-twigs and piss around her house. They ex-communicate the mother and the son and deny them even the labour work in the village leading to their starvation. These forms of settlements and punishments are still in vogue in rural India.

Advised by his mentor in the town, Kakka boldly sets about improving things for his mother by suitably getting her remarried, though she refuses initially. He fixes her remarriage with a widower from a neighbouring village, and gets her married.

In a second instance at the end of the novel, the *rachabanda* again stands as a symbol of injustice this time by the government. On account of the land dispute, Kakka is thrashed, wounded by the Reddy landlords. Kakka having been suffered insult and violence, and denied of medical treatment, an educated dalit college boy lodges a complaint and fights for justice. The government deputes an officer to examine the case. The officer, being sympathetic to the fellow dalits, conducts a court in the village. The officer, moved by the incident, becomes sympathetic towards the dalits. When the madigas demand for some land for raising huts, the officer concedes. Enraged by the decision, the landlords of the village manhandle and wound the officers, who leave the village without settling the dispute. The *rachabanda*, which is a slab, breaks signifying the failure of the state mechanism in delivering justice to the dalits. Ending inconclusively, the novel portrays the socio-political scenario of the Telangana region dealing with the conspiracy of Visalandhra and the atrocities of Reddy and Kamma landlords and Nizam's Razakars.

Madigirkam: Productive Culture

Kakka grows fond of learning *madigirkam*, the caste occupation. He dreams of rendering the service of madigirkam to the landlords, and befriends an old man by name Pakeerthaatha, who helps him become a farm hand to a *dora*, an upper caste landed gentry. During the nights, Kakka works hard to master madigirkam, which includes drum-beating, tanning, making and mending sandals and making agricultural leather items. He works hard to learn them all with a view to undertaking caste profession. But to his dismay, he learns that he is not entitled to the caste profession as he hails from a negligible 'sect' of madigas in the village. Kakka feels humiliated on account of discrimination within his community. He considers it oppression by his caste men. He questions the exploitation, discrimination and intra-rivalries of the madiga community.

Sub-sects within Madigas

Convinced by Kakka's sincerity and hard work, Pakeerthaatha, who belongs to a different sect of the madigas, comes forward to offer him in marriage his granddaughter, Lasmakka in spite of resistance by the people of his sect. Arrangements for the marriage are afoot. When the women try to fetch *puttammannu*, anthill clay, a requirement in the wedding ritual, the landed gentry instigate the sudras to attack the madigas brutally on the day of Kakka's wedding. However, they complete the wedding ritual by fetching the anthill clay from a different place. After the wedding, when the madigas take the bride and the groom around the village in a procession, the landlords and the sudras thrash them mercilessly. In a third incident, when the landlords and sudras beat the madigas again, the latter retaliate by beating them back.

Agrarian and Power Relations

One of the landlords obtains on a blank paper the signature of Pakeerthaatha, to lodge a police complaint against the madigas. The landlords earlier made Pakeerthaatha *sarpanch*, the president of the village without the knowledge of anyone, including Pakeerthaatha. The police take all the madiga men into custody, and harass them in the Station. Pakeerthaatha, unable to bail out the madigas, commits suicide considering himself responsible for the disputes involving his caste men.

Meanwhile, the madigas reconcile themselves to the changing circumstances in the village. The farmhands are replaced by daily-wage workers. The local landlords let out the land on tenancy, and sell some of it to the migrant coastal farmers, who cultivate commercial crops replacing the conventional paddy and grains denying the labourers the food grains.

Disturbed by the disputes, and to overcome weariness, the madiga youth plan to perform a street play, because the professional cindu players refused, being earlier denied of the patronage of the madigas because of draught. Kakka is chosen for the lead role in a play called '*Mahisasura Vadha*' (assassination of Mahisasura) which deals with competing for supremacy between the gods and the demons. Kakka's wife resists him from playing the role as she finds the story similar to the incidents taking place in their village. Yet Kakka rehearses his role – the song and the action – with determination. When they get ready to enact the play, Kakka goes out to relieve himself, and has been whisked away by a group of unknown masked persons. They batter him and slit open his calf muscles causing wounds. They made him incapacitated preventing him from playing the role.

Centering the Linguistic Marginality

The novel is written in a language that had been marginalised. By doing so, the writer aims at centering the language that was considered unworthy of literature earlier.

Yellaiah uses many aspects of linguistic marginalisation. Dalit literature being defiant deviates from the forms of the mainstream literature. *Kakka* is a step ahead in defiance of and deviation from the modern Telugu dalit literature. The main defiance of *Kakka* lies in its deviation even from the dalit writing in respect of the style and the language that Yellaiah chooses in his novels. His effort is to reclaim, to privilege, to centre the dalit language.

The first aspect of defiance is the use of Telangana dialect both in the dialogue and narrative. However, it is not a new experiment to write a novel entirely in the Telangana dialect. Other writers who used dialect in fiction include Dasharadhi Rangacharya in Telangana; Raavi Saastri in coastal Andhra; and Namini Subrahmanyam Nayudu in Rayalaseema. The use of the dialect in their novels received alround acclaim since they belong to upper castes. But *Kakka* failed to evoke same kind of response among the mainstream readers for Yellaiah goes ahead of these writers in respect of register and mode.

To enrich the Telangana dialect, Yellaiah uses for the first time, the madiga register. On this count, *Kakka* is the first of its kind in Telugu dalit literature. The portrayal of the madiganess – tanning, making leather goods, dappu-beating, rendering agricultural services; cultural aspects like the rituals of birth, death, wedding, puberty, eating bullock-meat, devadasi system and sindus' street plays – are rendered using madiga register as they are culture specific; madiga specific.

Yellaiah complements the Telangana dialect and madiga register with the use of the oral form. The novel is not written in the written mode but in the spoken mode – the orality. This is in keeping with the illiteracy of the dalit characters and situations in the novel.

Most of the Telugu letters that Yellaiah uses are not 'acceptable' in the written mode. He has successfully avoided the use of the allophones (k^h, g^h, ch^h, j^h, t^h, d^h, th^h, dh^h, p^h and b^h), which are characteristic of written mode; which are hardly used in speech even by the educated speakers. Further, Yellaiah also avoided the use of post-alveolar '*n*', '*l*'. The writer would say that they cannot be overcome overnight, and would ask, "How can Telugu dalit literature come of age without overcoming the Sanskritic post-alveolar /l/ in 'da*l*it', which the dalits themselves cannot pronounce?" (343).

The next aspect of Kakka is about neologisms. Most of the words Yellaiah uses are not free morphemes. Several words he uses are not lexical in the sense that they cannot be found in the dictionaries; they do not exist in isolation. They need to be understood as separate words forming a new word. He would inflect or derive novel forms of words by strangely joining together separate words. The joining of the words is accomplished in a different way. This aspect of combining the words is characteristic of orality. By doing so Yellaiah creates a new genre of the novel that could be termed *shravya navala*, an audio-novel to be read aloud.

True to the oral mode, the novelist breaks the rules of grammar of the written Telugu. The dexterity of the novelist is demonstrated in the style, which is different from the written but familiar to the spoken mode. Another unique feature of the narrative is doing away with punctuation, especially commas, quotes for dialogues and full stops. The avoidance of the punctuation allows the flow of narration in the manner of dalit street-play called *Sindukatha* and *Yakshagaanam*; in the manner of an illiterate's speech.

His experiments with the Telangana dialect, madiga register, morphology and syntax are aimed at legitimating the dalit language. *Kakka* is, thus, a deviation even from the contemporary Telugu dalit literature on three fronts – the dialect, the register and the orality. The reclaiming of the dalit language through the stylistic experiments is but dalitising Telugu by liberating it from the Sanskritic influence. A dalitised art form would have to be produced as an anti-thesis of and in opposition to the conventional art form. This is accomplished in defying all the established and known forms and world views of the conventional art. As defiance is the crux of dalit protest, defiance of the conventional art-forms forms the core of dalit literature.

References

Yellaiah, Vemula. *Kakka.* Nalgonda: Gosangi Prachuranalu, 2000. Translated by K. Purushotham and Gita Ramaswami, and the English version is yet to be published.

—. "Our Exit from the left was the Beginning of the Dalit Writing." interviewed by K. Purushotham and J. Bheemaiah, *Journal of Literature and Aesthetics.* Vol. 9, No. 1&2 (Jan-Dec 2009). Print.

5

A Leftist's Dalit Novel: Kalyana Rao's *Untouchable Spring*[1]

Gopal Guru classifies Marathi dalit writers into two categories: the elitist and the mudhouse writers. The former, according to him aspire to be acceptable to and assimilatable into the canonical writings of various hues including the Left. The latter aim at radicalising the dalit masses through 'cultural assertion from below' (187). This paradigm can be applied to the Telugu dalit writing too. Some of the contemporary Telugu dalit writers use the ethos and language of the dalits without stylising and having to conform to any of the literary elements of the canonical literature. They are putting in sincere efforts at the cultural assertion from below. However, some of the Telugu dalit writings are modeled after the canonical works conforming to the tenets of the mainstream literature.

Kalyana Rao's *Untouchable Spring* is a case in point. It is a dalit novel consisting of dalit characters, dealing with the problem of untouchability, encompassing a hundred years of dalit life. One of the reviews reads, "*Antarani Vasantam* addresses the issue of untouchability experienced by six generations of people...The socio-cultural life, humiliations and oppression by the forward castes and other related issues are discussed in a scientific manner" (27). Published by *Virasam*, a frontal literary organisation that represents the ideology of the extreme Left, the novel received wide acclaim selling in good numbers. The novelist is an ideologue of the extreme Left. Without defying the conventional narrative technique, the novel is modeled after the conventional novel in two aspects: the European form and the Leftist world view.

The novel does not defy the conventions of a well-made novel. The crux of a dalit novel lies in dalitisation, of the form and the content. The European form needs to be given up for the dalit street-plays and ballets. The content of a dalit novel springs from the dalit-specific repression, discrimination and the concomitant dalit-specific reaction. As regards the content, *Untouchable Spring* can be considered a dalit novel till the end of chapter twelve, exactly half the novel. The remaining half reads like a class-based novel advocating violence and revolution like Vattikota Alwarswamy's *Prajalamanishi* (The Man of the People) and *Vasanthageetham* (The Muse of Spring) of anonymous authorship.

A quick perusal of the history of Telugu dalit literature would enable one locate this novel in proper perspective. The Telugu dalit literature runs parallel to the dalit movement in Andhra Pradesh. The early period, which may be termed the reformative phase was marked by the Bhakti writings of Potuluri Veerabrahmam and Vemana. The Adi-Andhra movement that held its first conference in 1917 under the leadership of Bhagya Reddy Verma faded in the 1930s when the Nationalist movement began under the leadership of Gandhi, who visited Andhra in 1932-33. Gurram Jashuva, Boyi Bheemanna and others, who began to write under the influence of Gandhi's Harijan upliftment, continued to write in the following phase that may be said to have commenced in 1944, when Ambedkar visited Krishna district in Andhra Pradesh. These writers, especially Jashuva, were ignored in the literary historiography (Satyanarayana 99).[2] The next phase of Telugu dalit literature commenced in 1985, the year in which the notorious atrocities of the upper castes against the dalits in Karamchedu, and later at other places took place. This period marks the beginning of the new phase of the dalit literature. The writings of this period could be rightly termed the *dalit phase*. The works produced by the second and third generation educated dalits, who subscribe themselves to the ideology of Ambedkar, question the role of the Left in the dalit emancipation. It may not be out of place to state that the dalit discourse in politics and literature strengthened ever since the dalits began to deviate from the Left in Andhra Pradesh.

Untouchable Spring, written in the third phase, subscribes instead to the Leftist ideology. The narration opens with the introduction of Ruth, a sixth generation urban Christian character in the lineage of the women in the novel. The narration traces out the history of the lives of the dalits encompassing a hundred years, consisting of the pre- and the post-Independence period. Ruben takes over the narration by the end of the novel. Both the narrators – Ruth and the omniscient narrator – are aliens to the dalit 'insiders.' Ruth, through whose eyes the reader gets to know the life of the dalits, is alien because she is born and brought up in the urban milieu with Christian background, and therefore she would perceive the problems of the dalits with sympathy and pity, which the dalits have outgrown in reality. And the novelist in the form of the omniscient narrator too is an outsider in the novel because he would view the dalits, in his capacity as the omniscient narrator, critically as an onlooker, observer and judge. As the one, who knows the motives behind every thought and deed of the characters, he would maintain equidistance.

The narrative technique is not inclusive of the dalit art forms. The 'outsider-narration' disables the novelist from having an account of the experience of the dalits at personal and collective level. The main thrust of the dalit literature is on their personal experiences as well as the experiences of their ancestors based on memory. The experience of the dalits only gets expressed with a sympathetic treatment by the narrators. The narrators unwittingly assume the role of considering the subjects as the Other; as writing on behalf of them, but not the characters writing about themselves. The illiterate characters as they are: Sinasubbadu, Ellanna, Errenkadu, Sivaiah; and the women,

Sinasubbi, Lachimi, Lingalu, Subhadra and Sasirekha in that order, excepting Ruth and Ruben, could have 'written' themselves using the rich dalit oral art forms. Ruth, Ruben and the narrator, being educated, make sweeping generalisation on art and literature. As a result, the narrative often becomes polemical and pedantic. The narrator's observations on art, aesthetics and agrarian relations are well informed to the educated. This amounts to intellectualisation of the dalit life. The analyses of their lives seem superimposed. Moreover, such an attempt is tantamount to considering the characters ignorant and inferior as against their inherent elements of protest and revolt.

Ruth, like the novelist himself, is a creative writer, educated, liberated and urban-born and brought up. She learns about the dalit life through the memories of her husband, Ruben. There are similarities between Ruth, the non-participant persona and the all-pervasive narrator. Both of them are educated, non-participant observers and aestheticians. They does the role of reformers/liberators of sorts. They are distanced in time and place from their subjects. They are in a sense alienated from those that they are writing about. As a result, both Ruth and the narrator self-consciously project that they are what they are not; that they empathise with their subjects.

Then comes the style, which too does not defy the style of a conventional novel. The novel is written in: (a) the mode of written language, which is in opposition to the illiteracy of the dalits; (b) the 'acceptable' or 'received' Telugu least affected by the dialects of the locale of the novel i.e. Rayalaseema and the coastal region; (c) keeping the dialogue to the least minimum possible; and (d) the non-dalit sociolect. The novel lacks in the caste specific phonology (the sounds of words), morphology (the inflections uniquely used by the dalits), syntax (the mal-formed) – not well-formed – word order. The dalit narrative and the dalit dialogue cannot take place in a stylised language. Structuralist linguists like Sossure would hold that written mode corrupts the language, and that the oral mode is the most authentic form of the language. The oral dalit dialect can best communicate the dalit experience. Vemula Yellaiah in *Kakka,*

Endluri Sudhakar in *Mallemoggala Godugu* and the short story writers like Nagappagari Sunderraj, Jupaka Subhadra, Jajula Gowri, Gogu Shyamala, Kalekuri Prasad and Nallala Laxmirajam use the dalit language and oral tradition in their writings communicating the authenticity from below.

Equally important factor that negates the element of dalitisation in the novel is the typology of the most important character, Yellaiah. The main thrust of the novel begins and ends with the birth and the death of Yellaiah, without many struggles on his part. Yellaiah is portrayed as a picaro as well as Kunstllerroman – portrait of the growth of an artist. Yellaiah is the grandfather of Ruth's husband, Ruben. The reader learns about Yellaiah through Ruth-Ruben account provided by the narrator. Yellaiah experiences in his childhood both physical and mental trauma on account of untouchability. Chased by the caste-Hindus, Yellaiah by chance runs into a dalit artist under whose training, he grows into an artist of repute. Then on, Yellaiah becomes a *Bhairagi,* an Indian version of a picaro learning and spreading the song in the region leaving behind his son, Sivaiah and wife, Subhadra. By the fag end of his life, he would however return to his village, Enneladinni, the locale of the novel, during the famine, and dies on joining his wife and the grown up son. This part of the story running into half of the novel consists of the dalit experience – the untouchability, the agrarian relations, the atrocities, the inter and the intra-caste relations in the village, transition of the villages – all of which subject the Malas and the Madigas to abject poverty, insults and repression. But, there is a problem with the typology of the character, Yellaiah.

The very premise of dalit life is based on the work culture, and here is a character, who wanders performing ballets and songs leaving behind his wife and son. Yellaiah's alienation from work (he is sporadically shown to be working during his wandering) and his embracing of art as a mission is an instance of leisurely pursuit of art. There is a sustained attempt of valorising Yellaiah, the artist and his art. In valorising so, the novelist's attempt is to create a parallel art of the dalits in opposition to the mainstream classical art forms. Every sub-caste has constructed a form of art and it is practiced exclusively as an occupation without regular work. They depend on their art for survival. *Untouchable Spring* has one such character by name Naganna, who survives on art. Naganna trains Yellaiah, who also becomes an art professional. This very attempt of exclusivist art without a productive occupation is characteristic of Brahminical way of life evading work and hardships of life. This aspect needs to be dalitised, and instead of doing so, the narrator glorifies the kinds of Naganna and Yellaiah, the latter earning the epithet, Atelladu-Patelladu (Singer-Elladu and Ballet-Elladu). The novelist focuses on the development of Yellaiah as an artist, but in the process creates an escapist character – escape from family and partially from work. In the process of his pursuit of art, Yellaiah becomes a Bhairagi. Yellaiah, who otherwise would have been a wonderful dalit character, has been ruined as a dalit character because of his being modeled on Kunstullerroman and picaro.

Every dalit caste of the region has at least one dependent community, who survive by begging through art. Artists belonging to these communities, who are still prevalent, thrive on art, but not on work. Most of the artists within the dalit community do not take part in productive work. Any form of institutionalised art assumes its leisurely practice providing the escapist rout. Besides, Yellaiah's irresponsibility towards family for whatever reason is non-dalit and Sanskritic in sacrificing work and family in pursuit of art. The pursuit of the underground activities in the M.L politics by abandoning work and family is akin to the Brahminical renunciation of family in pursuit of truth by the saints.

Yellaiah's death gives an abrupt turn to the story. There is a shift in the thrust of the novel from the caste to the class struggle. The narrator prepares the reader, right from the beginning of the second half, for a solution in the class-based struggles. Dalitisation primarily lies in finding a solution within the parameters of caste. As K.G. Satyamurthy noted, the working classes have the potential to create a classless society, the suppressed castes too are potential enough to create a casteless society. Ambedkar has adequately established the inability of the former in the context of a caste-based society like India. In fact, the reason for the delay or the slow-paced dalitisation is the prevalence of the class-based polity both in the mainstream and the underground polity. Ironically, as delineated in the later part of the novel, the cadre of the Left is drawn essentially from the dalit communities thereby assimilating the dalits into its fold distancing them from any possibility of dalitisation. The thirteenth chapter onwards, the novel runs at a faster pace. Yellaiah's grandchildren, Ruth and Ruben and great grandchildren, Mary Suvartha, Emmanuel, Jessy and Ruby work as cadre in the underground Left. Ruben would ruminate, like Gorky's Mother, the struggle and sacrifice of her progeny, and derives fulfillment out of it. The second half of the novel runs insipidly carrying out polemics of class struggles, glorifying sacrifice, bloodshed and so on contrary to the vibrancy and the volatility of the dalit life. Thus, the second half of the novel reminds one of *Vasantha Geetham*, a novel of anonymous authorship. Though familiar with the dalit emotions, aspirations and living conditions, Kalyana Rao's portrayal of the dalit life is informed by his Marxist ideology. This aspect is characteristic of the dalit literature written by the *savarna*, non-dalit writers as interpreted by a noted historian, Adapa Satyanarayana. (94)

In terms of history, the class-based militant struggles may be realistic in parts of Andhra Pradesh. But there is other side of it too. Most of the people who lost their lives in the militant struggles were the dalits, whose children are deprived of parents; wives deprived of husbands. What is noteworthy is that besides the militant struggles, there have been dalit movements in Andhra Pradesh in the form of attacking the social constructs of oppression. But the dalit movements were overshadowed by the Left. The novel is silent on this very important aspect of social transformation.

Dalits in India are, thus, subjected to assimilation even in the modern period. The Church lured them in the name of Missionary education and health leading to large scale conversions. The dalit Christians suffered double alienation in the Church: from the European Christians and the upper caste Christians. The problem of the untouchability continued in the Church too. Subsequently, the dalits were organised socially and politically under the banner of *Adi-Andhra*, sons of the soil movement during the period 1917-1940 by Bhagya Reddy Verma. But the Nationalist movement fizzled out the dalit movement incorporating the dalits in the guise of Gandhi's Harijan upliftment sidelining the issue of the caste and untouchability. The third betrayal of the dalits this time around is by the Left which has been roping in the dalits into their cadre without addressing the issues of caste and untouchability so fundamental to the lives of the dalits. It is in this sense that Chinna Rao Yagati, a historian describes the political predicament of the dalits aptly, "Dalits were used, abused and politicised by all political parties, Congress, Communist and non-Brahman"(139). The aspect of the dalit assimilation into the Right, the Left and the Christianity has been abundantly represented in the Telugu novel.[3] The dalits have been affirmative in respect of protest, defiance and culture which need to be explored by the historians, political scientists and writers. Against this background, Kalyana Rao's *Untouchable Spring* best fits into a sub-genre that may be termed the revolutionary dalit novel.

References

Chinna Rao, Yagati. *Dalits' Struggle for Identity*, New Delhi: Kanishka Publishers, Distributors, 2003. Print.

Guru, Gopal. "The Interface Between Ambedkar and the Dalit Cultural Movement in Maharastra." Ed. Ghanshyam Shah, *Dalit Identity and Politics: Subordination and the Dalit Challenge*, Vol. 2, New Delhi: Sage Publications, 2001. Print.

Kalyana Rao, G. *Untouchable Spring*. Trans. Alladi Uma and Sreedhar. Hyderabad: Orient BlackSwan, 2006. Print.

Satyanarayana, A. "Dalit Protest Literature in Telugu: A Historical Perspective." *Dalits and Uppercastes: Essays in Social History*. New Delhi: Kanishka Publishers, Distributors, 2005. Print.

Satyanarayana, K. "The Discovery of Jashua: The Shaping of Dalit Literary Tradition in Telugu." *Language Forum*, Vol. 33, No. 1. Jan-June 2007: 99-111. Print.

Thirumala Rao, Jayadhir. "*Antarani Vasantam.*" *The Book Review* (February 2002). Print.

Notes

1. An earlier version of this paper was presented at a three-day national seminar on "Personal Narratives of Dalits and their Religion(s)" organised by the School of Humanities, Department of English, University of Hyderabad, Hyderabad, October 16 – 18, 2007.

2. It is interesting to note that writers of all hue have sidelined Jashua. The Rightwing neo-classicists brushed aside Jashua and they projected the Hindu Dharma as a solution to all the problems. The Leftwing critics like Chalasani Prasadrao, Chenchaiah and K. V. Ramana Reddy had written off Jashua as a traditionalist for not using the free verse.

3. Novels dealing with the themes of assimilation of the dalits into the Right, the Left and the Christianity, written at different points of time include, Tallapragada Suryanarayana Rao's *Helavati* (1913), Venkataparvateesh-wara Kavulu's *Matrumandiram* (1919), Unnava Laxmi-narayana's *Malapalli* (1920, Acharya Ranganaya-kulu's *Harijana Nayakuldu* (1933), Adavi Bapiraju's *Narudu* (1946), Ilindra Ranganayakulu's *Mallika* (1950), Vattikota Alwarswami's *Prajalamanishi* (1955), Muppala Ranganaya-kamma's *Balipeetham* (1962), Maheedara Rammohana Rao's *Kollayigattitenemi* (1965), Malladi Vasundara's *Trivarna Pataka* (1965), Vachaspati's *Anthasthulu–Anthahkaranalu* (1965), Dasharathi Rangacharya's *Chillaradevullu* (1970), Kesava Reddy's *Banisalu* (1971) and *Shmashanam Dunneru* (1979), *Incrdible Goddess* (1979), and Illendula Saraswati's *Neebanchenu Kallumokkuta* (1976). Most of these novels, written by the *savarnas*, do not represent the cultural assertion of the dalit life and language.

6

Dalit Short Stories: From Elite To Mud-House Narratives

Dalit poetry in Telugu is above hundred years old; but short fiction took fairly a long time to be what it is now. Shaped by the literary and social movements, the Telugu dalit short fiction traversed a long way in transforming itself from elite to mud-house both in language and content. This article maps the phases in the rise of the dalit short fiction in Telugu.

The Pre-Dalit Phase

The first phase of the Telugu dalit short fiction, written by the upper castes, is in two strands: the short story from the Telangana and the Andhra regions.

Authors from the latter wrote under the influence of the nationalist movement. In pursuance of the Gandhian motto of 'harijan upliftment,' and against the conversions to Christianity and Islam, they criticised the practice of untouchability and espoused humanism. "Pallamraju," the first ever dalit story by a non-dalit was written by Sripada Subramanya Shastry in 1925 criticising the conversions. However, the same author wrote another story later on suggesting the conversions as a viable solution. Other non-dalit writers, who wrote on the dalits, include Chinta Dikshitulu, Karuna Kumara, N.G. Ranga and Doma Venkatagupta Swami, among others. Their writings reflect such concerns as untouchability, temple entry, discouraging conversions, inhumanity, exploitation and inter-caste marriages invoking pity and sympathy. The stories are written with sympathy for the dalits without reflecting the conflicts, self-respect, affirmation of dalit culture and protest. The non-dalit writers in the subsequent period wrote on exploitation and the failure of the State in transforming dalits' lives. Concerning language, they used the 'standard' idiom, which may be due to their social configuration and regional background.

Short fiction from the Telangana region was shaped by the peasants' armed struggle (1946-51) against the jagirdars and deshmukhs, who were ruling *samsthanams*, villages. The concern of the writers was anti-feudal, and was written in dialect as against the 'standard' variety. The writers include Ayodhya Ramakavi, Vattikota Alwaruswami, Kaloji Narayana Rao, Suravaram Pratapa Reddy and others beginning from 1943 to the end of the armed struggle. There are at least a dosen anthologies of short stories (individual and collections) on the armed struggle and an anthology on the nationalist movement in Telangana edited by Devulapalli Ramunuja Rao. In the later period, B.S. Ramulu's "Chaduvu," (education) Sannapureddi Venkatrami Reddy's, "Antu" (pollution) and "Chanubalu" (breast milk), Toleti Jasganmohan Rao's "Kulam" (caste), Allam Rajaiah's "Madhyavarthulu," (mediators), Shanti Narayana's "Ukkupadam," (steel foot) and Kaluva Mallaia's "Vairudhyalu" (contradictions) critically deal with the question of caste and untouchability.

In both the regions, the dalit question did attract the attention of the authors, though they were drawn more towards the nationalist struggle in Andhra and land struggles in Telangana. Both the movements, however, did not benefit the dalits. The stories depict the poverty of the dalits.

The Epochal Shift

Because of the rise in literacy and awareness, a shift has taken place in the genre. Ranga Rao writes: "with the spread of education and the democratic spirit, writers in impressive numbers have started coming from the other two regions" (261). Their stories are remarkable for the use of the dialect and the depiction of the struggles for economic equality.

Writers from the west Rayalaseema, K. Shobha, Madhuranthakam Rajaram, Krishna Reddy, V.R. Rasani, Kesava Reddy and Namini Subramanyam Naidu; and from the northern Telangana Allam Rajaiah, B.S. Ramulu, Boya Jangaiah, Thummeti Ragotham Reddy, Jukanti Jagannatham and others wrote in their respective dialects as different from their counterparts in the coastal region. In the subsequent period, there has been an 'epochal shift' (Rao, 227) in the direction of representing the regional ethos of the Telangana and the Rayalaseema regions, which are known for backwardness. The Telugu short fiction underwent a transition when the writers of the two backward regions questioned the formation of the coastal writing as the canon, and affirmed the use of the dialects, which are regional in character. The regionalisation of the genre thus legitimised the use of the dialects effecting a shift from the centre to the margins.

The writers of these regions dealt with poverty and exploitation leading to the formation of the 'movement literature' in the second half of the twentieth century. *Abhyudaya Rachayithala Sangham* (ARASAM) Progressive Writers' Association (1935-55) and *Viplava Rachayithala Sangham* (VIRASAM), Revolutionary Writers' Association (1970-80) too pursued the themes of land struggles and class- based perception of exploitation refusing to consider caste as an important source of social subordination and marginalisation. VIRASAM published quite a few anthologies of short stories focussing on land and class struggles without addressing the caste question.

Another socio-literary movement that neglected caste as well as the land struggles was the feminist movement. With a long tradition of women's writing, confirmed feminist short story writers like Volga, Sathyavathi, Kuppili Padma and others wrote powerfully on the domestic and social violence without questioning the caste and religious bases of the Indian patriarchy.

Against the backdrop of the neglect (by the short story writers belonging to the armed struggle, the nationalist, progressive, revolutionary and feminist movements) of the caste as the source of subordination, the dalit short fiction was taking a definitive shape. Dalits were active during these non-caste movements with parallel movements of their own; writings of their own. The first ever anthology of Telugu dalit short stories, *Dalita Kathalu* (1996), edited by Chandrasekhar Reddy and Laxminarayana is an important milestone in the emergence of the genre. Among the twenty-five authors in the volume, Kolakaluri Enoch, Chilukuri Devaputra and Boya Jangaiah are dalits, the rest upper castes. The significance of the anthology is that it was the first ever compilation in Telugu to have come with the title, *Dalita Kathalu*. It raised consciousness about the caste among the educated dalit students, scholars and writers. Besides this, Laxminarayana brought out seven volumes of short stories written between 1910 and 1998. Classified into sub-themes, the volumes contain one-fifth of the stories by the dalits and the rest by the others.

Though small in number, the dalit writing marks a shift from being written about to writing themselves. There has been a debate on the question of representation: writing oneself and being written about by the others. The latter is about the witnessed or observed reality and the former represents the experienced reality, which is known as the historical dalitness.

Historical Dalitness

Historical dalitness in sociological terms is narrating one's dalitness by birth. It took ten years for the dalits from being written about (first in 1925 by Sripada) to writing themselves in 1935. This genre began with the emergence of the educated dalits, and the first story of this genre, "Ayyopapam" (alas!) was written in 1935 by Gottumukkala Mangayamma, a dalit woman. Kolakaluri Enoch's "Dikkulenodu" (an orphan) was based on the burning of a dalit boy by name Kotesh in 1965 followed by

"Oorabaavi" (public-well) published in 1969. The latter, considered a landmark story, deals with the problem of drinking water, chastity of dalit women and struggle for self-respect. A dalit woman slaps an upper caste man for his misbehaviour. When the upper castes deny drinking water in vengeance, her husband Chidambram dumps a dead animal into the well. When Chidambaram and his father were thrashed and tied in the village junction, his wife fights heroically and saves them. The story drives home the point that the laws do not protect the dalits. The bold deed of a dalit woman may be understood in contrast to the passive and docile women of the upper castes. In another story of Enoch, "Godda Donga" (cattle thief), Nagadu, who lives on butchery, is accused of stealing the cattle. Keeping vigil in the night, Nagadu catches red-handed the real culprit, who is none other than an upper caste *dora*, landlord of the village. Thinking that the dora will be let off due to his social status, Nagadu kills him, stuffs the body into the stomach of an ox and throws into water. When the actual cattle thief was exposed, the theft of the cattle stops. Enoch depicts in the story how the doras brand the madigas as cattle thieves.

A tradition thus started, several other dalit writers penned short stories radically different from those of the non-dalit writers. Boya Jangaiah, Chilukuri Devaputra, Paidi Tereshbabu, Madduri Nageshbabu, Kalekuri Prasad and Gundedappu Kanakaiah, among others wrote stories of dissent and protest. Boya jangaiah, who began writing from the Marxist perspective, published several anthologies of dalit short stories with depth and insights. In "Kolupulu" (the idols), the protagonist Enkulu ekes out his life by breaking stones at the nearby hillock; they live by selling stones. Enkulu carves in his leisure time a figure of monkey on one of the stones. Then he smears *kumkum*, vermilion on it, and begins to worship it. He makes the others in the village worship it treating it as the idol of lord Hanuman. The shrine becomes very popular in the neighbourhood. Suddenly the temple committee replaces Enkulu by a brahmin priest on the grounds that he is illiterate and cannot recite slokas. Finding no justice from the officials, one day he blasts the shrine as a sign of protest. His wife, Durgamma's non-superstitious attitude is noteworthy. She says when at work with the stones: 'The neem-tree can't be the deity nor a stone be the god. You [stone] are the only source of livelihood to people like us.' Stories of this kind radically differ from the ones written by non-dalite in the treatment of the themes.

Defiance of Form

The first generation dalit writing, however, did not radicalise the language and technique: concerning language, they did not go beyond the use of the dialect; regarding the technique, they imitated the canonical well-made structure of the story. The new generation dalit writers, in stark contrast, radicalised the genre by using the dalit register. Instead of the well-made form, they employed the style of narrativising the experiences blurring the difference between autobiographical and fictional narrative.

Their target readers not being the complaisant middle classes, the radical dalit writers did not aim at acceptability, but affirmation of their culture, ritual and identity. They used the oral tradition making use of the diction and register, which would otherwise be described as 'vulgar and obscurantist' (Dangle, 50) by the literary establishment. The radical dalit writers considered it a form of cultural assertion from below. This kind of writing entails "the double task of tackling the dalit literary establishment, on the one hand, and colonising the state, on the other." (Guru, 192)

The instances of defiance assumed extreme proportions of being unintelligible to the readers from the rest of the regions; and speakers of the non-dalit register. Vemula Yellaiah's stories and novels, *Kakka* (2000) and *Siddi* (2004) invoked criticism on the grounds that his prose is difficult to read. Besides the Telangana dialect, Yellaiah uses the register as used in the madiga environs. The credit for beginning a new genre, which is termed 'mud-house' writing as against the 'elite' writing (Guru) may be attributed to Yellaiah. Other writers from Telangana include Gogu Shyamala, Jupaka Subhadra and Kadire Krishna. Their counterpart in Rayalaseema is late

Nagappagari Sunder Raju. He wrote "Nadiminti Bodekka Basiviralayyeda," which deals with the practice of *basivi / jogini*, initiating dalit women into prostitution. The story is equally beyond the grasp of the uninitiated reader.

The writers of this genre defend their language on the grounds that it is close to the language actually spoken by the dalits. They prefer the mud-house language at the expense of intelligibility. When asked about a writer's preference between intelligibility and representation, Yellaiah avers: "Dalit writer has to prefer representation to intelligibility. Cultural representation cannot be sacrificed for readability. The difficulties that readers might face can be overcome by effort. But if representation is sacrificed for intelligibility, it amounts to erasing one's own culture and identity...culture is best transmitted by one's own register and dialect. (Yellaiah, 343)

By choosing to write in the mud-house language, the Telugu dalit short story mirrors the dalit middle classes and the lower classes, a feature that does not characterise the Gujarati Dalit short stories as observed by Rita Kothari.

Women Writers

Dalit women short fiction is remarkable for varied reasons. Men's short fiction had to pass through several phases: in the first phase, they were written about by the upper castes during the nationalist and peasants' armed struggle; in the second phase, their own writing was, in the beginning, imitative of the elite writing; most of them are yet to use dalit register and defy the form; they are yet to write on the dependant castes.

In contrast, the dalit women's stories came of age on the above four scores without having to pass through as many phases. The elite feminists did not write about the dalit women; without having to be written about by the upper caste feminists, dalit women wrote about themselves. Unlike their men counterparts, the dalit women did not imitate the writings of the elite feminist writings. Regarding the defiance of form, the dalit women writers are decisively ahead of their men counterparts in the use of the dialect, register and defiance of structure/technique. Most importantly, the dalit women are writing on the women belonging to the dependent castes.

Beginning with *Nallapoddu* (dark sunrise), an anthology of dalit women's writing, published in 2004 traces the tradition of dalit women's writing from 1921 to 2002. This anthology, though most of the selections do not reflect dalit or gender perspectives, could be considered a dalit response to *Neelimeghalu* (1993), an anthology of poetry by elite feminists, which failed to include dalit women writers. However, considering that *Nallapoddu* suffered from limitations that it represents mainly the mala as well as coastal writers, another anthology, *Nallaregati Saallu* (furrows of black soil), stories on madiga and its sub-castes, was published in 2006. Both the anthologies focused the dalit women writers hitherto neglected in the anthologies, historiography, syllabus and research. The dalit women intelligentsia in the last decade contributed to the emergence of dalit feminism by offering sharp critique of the exclusivist, elite feminism.

Jupaka Subhadra, Gogu Shyamala, Jajula Gowri, M.M. Vinodini, Challapalli Swarupa Rani, Sujatha Gidla, Jalli Indira, Putla Hemalatha, Kannaram Jhansi among others, have produced a considerable body of writing. Besides the literary genres like short story, poetry and personal/family narratives, a great deal of media-based debate on feminism has been taking place. The dalit writing and debates by women is sharp and more focused than the writings of their men counterparts: "the poetry by dalit women writing [sic] from the dalit women's perspective and based on their experiences as dalit women is far more powerful and has a far greater impact than the poetry of dalit male poets or upper caste women poets. Dalit women's issues have less in common with dalit men's issues than with those of the upper caste women." (Swaroopa Rani, 21) The dalit women's writing, thus, represents the concerns that are unique to themselves.

Jajula Gowri published *Mannu Buvva* (soil as food), an

anthology of remarkable stories about lives of dalit women labourers and the domestic and social violence on them. Gowri's "Kanche" (grasing ground) is a remarkable story in which a mother desists her teenage daughter from committing suicide for having been raped and conceived. Proposing to terminate her pregnancy, the mother reposes confidence in her daughter by asking her to lead a new life, which goes against the middle class morality: "'Here you listen, my daughter! I tell you bare truth! Your life is, more important for you than the sack of sin in your womb; the world around you; and even me! If one is alive, one can live forever washing the slush on one's body. I'll talk to the doctor-amma tomorrow itself; I'll get the sinful fetus dissipated,' saying so the mother guarded her daughter in her heart."

A Christian dalit writer and academic, Vinodini's "Maria," depicts how the two sisters face discrimination first in school, and their brahmin landlord at home. The story exposes how untouchability is practiced in public but not when it comes to sex. Mariya, raped by her brahmin landlord, commits suicide in shame. Her younger sister had already been raped by Venkateswarao's son. Mariya's sister does the unthinkable and confronts the upper caste landlord but of course to no avail. The vulnerability of dalit women is an important concern of Vinodini and other women writers.

One of the striking features of the dalits is the absence of patriarchy in the family. Chinna Rao, who worked on the dalits' struggle for identity writes: "In dalit culture, family and community relations are basically democratic in nature." (Chinna Rao, 42) Unlike in the Hindu family system, the men and the women of the madigas work on equal terms. The role-models of the mother, the servant maid and the sex object have no place in the dalit families. The dalit women, at times, exhibit more courage and expertise than the men; they work with men on equal par in rendering the manual labour. They play equal and active role in production (as labourers), decision-making in marriage, family, monetary and other matters. The extent of domestic violence against the dalit women is less when compared to their counterparts in the Hindu society. Their social institutions like marriage and family are not rigid and strait jacketed. Flexibility is what characterises the nature of the practices of the socio-religious institutions. The short stories by the dalit women reflect this aspect of the dalit patriarchy.

Dandora and After

The Dandora movement, launched in 1994 demanding for the rationalisation of reservations heralded a new epoch in the identity movement. Also known as the self-respect movement, dalits—especially the madigas—began to affirm for the first time their occupation of leather, eating of *eddu mamsam*, bullock meat, their language, culture, ritual practices, and the very name of their caste, 'madiga' being appended to their names like the upper caste Reddy, Shastri, Rao do. This signal achievement apart, the movement has changed the very course of the dalit writing where in there is a change in the language, thematic concerns and genres. A writer of Kolakaluri Enoch's stature acknowledged the influence of the Dandora movement on his later writings. The native elements or the 'little traditions' (Redfield) of the dalits earned respectability due to the Dandora movement. What characterises the madiga tradition is their occupation of the leatherwork, which is not undertaken by any other caste. Comparable to Chakkiliyas of the Tamil Nadu, Chamars of North India and Chambhars of Maharashtra, the main duty of the madigas is to cart the deceased cattle out of the village; cure the hide of the cattle; process the skin into fine leather; and sew sandals and various leather implements used in agriculture, irrigation and transport. Enoch, in one of the very interesting polemical stories, "Cheppulu" develops a conversation between a brahmin priest and a dalit, who argues about entering the sanctum sanctorum of the temple wearing cheppulu, and the priest refuses to allow him. Endluri Sudhakar also writes about cheppulu considering it a noble profession, and therefore worthy of worship. The authors in both the stories demand respect for the occupation of the madigas.

Besides the leatherwork, the madigas are the main source of farmhands to the landowning communities for which they are entitled to *mirasi*, rights of support and wages. They also render other services like cleaning the streets, notifying the villagers by oral announcements accompanied by the drumbeat and manual cleaning of the human excreta. For rendering these services, they may or may not get remuneration amounting to *etti*, bonded labour. The stories on the theme of etti abound in Telugu.

The madigas eat the meat of the pre-deceased bullocks, cows, and buffalos because of the affordability and nutritious values. On the occasions of ceremonies and festivals, they procure discarded/aged bullocks for feast meals. The eating of the bullock meat and leatherwork, having become the sources of their untouchability, the madigas are considered unsightly. Considered 'crude,' 'vulgar' and 'impolite', inferior to the malas, there is no marital relationship between madigas and malas, and among the madiga sub-castes. Being endogamous, they are autonomous and independent in terms of their economy, occupation and culture, which may be due to their exclusion from the mainstream society. The madiga caste "looks like [a] parallel full-fledged community within broad limits of Hindu society." (Reddy, 92)

One of the important features of the stories is the affirmation of what may be termed the dalit religion as different from Hinduism. The practices of rituals and conventions differ from region to region within the dalits, who pray the principle of *shakti* as manifest in the form of the female cult-deities of the family and caste. Their deities include, Kuntamma, Kolhapuramma, Batamma, Peddamma, Maisamma, Pochamma, Ellamma and Poleramma in different regions of the state. Unlike the Hindu mode of worship, the dalits do not worship the idols. The shakti-worship is mostly based on the formless images; not a definitive idol. For instance, the dalits worship Ellamma, Maisamma and her sub-cults; Pochamma and her sub-cults; and the famous biennial tribal *jatara*, fair of Sammakka-Sarakka in Telangana have neither definitive shape nor any idols. There are instances of worshipping the idols of Pochamma, which is because She is worshipped by the caste Hindus too, who might have introduced the convention of idol worship to Pochamma. All these aspects of the rituals are effectively portrayed in different stories.

Sub-Caste Stories

If the madigas and malas are in the margins, the remaining fifty seven dependent sub-castes (dependent castes) are outside the margins; in the peripheries of the village and the caste system having nothing to do with the rest of the communities in the villages. Assigned menial jobs, they live in sub-human conditions. Denied of literacy and any other rights, they are yet to write their castes and experiences. Just as it took several years for the madiga and mala writers to pen their experiences and achieve visibility, it is likely to take as many years for the remaining sub-castes to write their respective experiences, and be known as writers. This is certainly a shortcoming on the part of the Telugu dalit writing, and the tradition of denial of education is to be held responsible for keeping them outside literacy.

However, they are being written about by the malas and madigas. Jupaka Subhadra, one of the most prominent madiga women writers, penned a story, "Manyem" dealing with dakkalis, a nomadic dependant caste. Though they posses land, they are not supposed to cultivate it, and hence they give it to madigas in lieu of which the latter have to offer to the former *manyem*, fixed quantity of paddy. Because of draught or any other reasons, the dakkalis do not get manyem due to them. Denied of the paddy, Dakkali Rayakka in the story settles the scores between two madiga brothers, to whom the land was given, and delivers the judgment decisively, a feature uncommon among the elite women.

Gogu Shyamala's "Baindlame Bhoomadugada Mari," (doesn't the baindla woman demand for her land?) deals with baindla, a caste who live by performing priestly rituals to the madigas. In the story, Baindla Sayamma demands the landlord, who had expropriated her land, to give it back to her. Vemula Yellaiah's "Maila Kumkuma," (polluted kumkum) deals with yet another sub-caste known as madiga-mastins, who render carpentry and make *dappu*, drums to the madigas since the mainstream carpenters refuse to make agricultural implements for the madigas. "Block," Vinodini's story of stark realism, gives graphic description of a scavenger's work with human waste. The writer gives a moving account of *mahatar*, scavengers, a sub-caste of madigas. The desperation and hopelessness of Jilakaramma, the main character reminds one of naturalism.

The Telugu dalit writings in general represent the dalit ethos being historical in the sense of representing the historicity of oppression in optimistic and assertive terms as against what Eleanor Zelliot viewed the Marathi writings as "a little more pessimistic and dark in tone than…the dalit movement itself." (Zelliot viii) The Telugu dalit writings in general are not pessimistic; they represent the contemporary dalit movement. The aspects of representation and authenticity of the Telugu dalit literature are true to life. The dalit short story in Telugu is vibrant and seems more promising adding new anthologies and authors to the corpus of the genre year by year. However, what Gopal Guru observed about the retreating of the dalit cultural movement in Maharashtra, may partially be true of Andhra Pradesh because of academic orientation, quest for awards and literary recognition on the part of the writers.

Identity Writing

Cutting across the genres, dalit identity writing in Telugu emerged in the last decade. Yendluri Sudhakar's *Mallemoggala Godugu* (1999) meaning umbrella of jasmine buds, originally serialised in a Telugu daily, affirms the madiga occupation, culture and language. He portrays the conflicts and problems in madiga life. This book, known for introducing the genre of the autobiography, is an account of the experiences of the authors' friends and relations. Another book in the same genre is *Madigodu* (madiga man, 1997) by Nagappagari Sunder Raju, who portrays in it the deplorable condition of the madigas in Rayalasima region. Consisting of ten tales in a unique technique, the protagonist is unidentifiable, and could be the author himself. Delineating the life of a student, the tales present an adept youth in caste profession, education, skills and song. The author, who had succumbed to premature death, narrates in the stories the madiga culture. Another story, "Boddeddu Katha" portrays the consumption of the meat of pre-deceased animal as a great experience. D. Gopi's *Gudise Esobu Kathalu* (1992) is one more anthology dealing with personal experiences, but this time of the dalit Christians. Gopi, a practicing journalist from the coastal Andhra, narrates in highly readable prose, the snippets from the deplorable day-to-day experiences of malas and converted Christians, who suffer double humiliation: in the Church and the mainstream society.

References

Dangle, Arjun, ed. *No Entry for the New Sun: Translations from Modern Marathi Dalit Poetry*. New Delhi: Disha Books 1992. Print.

Guru, Gopal. "The Interface Between Ambedkar and the dalit Cultural Movement in Maharashtra." Ed. Ghanshyam Shah. *Dalit Identity and Politics: Cultural Subordination and the Dalit Challenge*, Vol. 2. New Delhi: Sage Publications, 2001. Print.

Kothari, Rita. "Short story in Gujarati Dalit Literature." *Economic and Political Weekly* (Nov. 30, 2001). Print.

Rao, Ranga. "Afterword." *That Man on the Road: Contemporary Telugu Short Fiction*. New Delhi: Penguin Books, 2006. Print.

Reddy, N.S. "Transitions in Caste Structures in Andhra Pradesh with Particular Reference to Depressed Castes," Ph. D Dissertation, Lucknow University, Lucknow. Ed Ghanshyam Shah. *Dalit Identity and Politics: Cultural Subordination and the Dalit Challenge*, Vol. 2. New Delhi: Sage Publications, 1992. Print.

Reddy, R. Chandrasekhar and Laxminarayana, K. *Dalitha Kthalau*. Hyderabad: Visalandhra, 1996. Print.

Shyamala, Gogu, ed. *Nalla Poddu* (black sun): *Dalita Streela Sahityam* 1921-2002. Hyderabad: Hyderabad Book Trust, 2004. Print.

Subhadra, Jupaka and Gogu Shyamala, ed. *Nalla Regati Saallu*. Hyderabad: Mysamma-Sabbanda Prachuranalu, 2006. Print.

Yagati, Chinnarao. *Dalits' Struggle for Identity*, New Delhi: Kanishka Publishers, Distributors, 1995. Print.

Yellaiah, Vemula. "Our Exit from the Left was the Beginning of Dalit writing." *Journal of Aesthetics and Literature.* 9:1 and 2 (Jan-Dec 2009). Print.

Zelliot, Eleanor. "A Bibliographic Essay." *From Untouchable to Dalit: Essays on the Ambedkar Movement,* New Delhi: Manohar, 2005. Print.

7

Telangana, Dalits, Land Rights: A Literary Perspective

It is important to examine how the dalits view the Leftist struggles for land as a conspiracy to deny land to the dalits. Dalits' engagement with the land question has been subjected to obliteration in the mainstream histories of socio-political movements in the erstwhile Andhra Pradesh. The Leftist slogan of *dunnevadide bhoomi*, land for the tillers, having been failed to benefit, the dalits in the Telangana villages have been engaged with struggles for land, for cultivating the land they owned and for watering their fields. The growth of the contemporary dalit movements across the country accounts for the failure of the Left in the deliverance of land, water and right to cultivate the land. Though land is a subject of empirical study, this paper takes into account the literary representations of dalits' relentless struggles for land rights and cultivation. Vemula Yellaiah's *Kakka*, Y.B. Satyanarayana's *My Father Baliah* and select short fiction are examined for the purpose. It is argued that the dalit writers deal with the caste as playing significant role in the denial of land, water and right to cultivate, the basic human rights.

The Left and the Land

Andhra Pradesh has been home for the Leftist movements, which created space for movements of extreme militancy to the moderate Left. The Left waged two major armed movements in Andhra Pradesh: the Telangana armed rebellion (1946-51) and the Srikakulam peasant uprising (1967-72). The Telangana movement, triggered by the murder of Doddi Komuraiah, turned into an armed rebellion, and subsequently became a guerilla movement. The movement entered into the villages in the form of *sangham*, associations with the village as a unit. The intensity of the rebellion continued till the arrival of the Union military.

Doddi Komuraiah was an activist of Andhra Maha Sabha (AMS), which had been established in 1930 primarily to save Telugu language and culture from the influences of Urdu and Muslim culture. The AMS expanded its activities to fight feudalism in Telangana as a part of which Komuraiah fought the landlords. In the process of fighting the landlords, he was shot by the private army of the notorious landlord, Visnoor Ramachandra Reddy. Following the murder, AMS waged an armed struggle against the *zamindars*, landlords.

Ramachandra Reddy used to own land in 60 villages, and his mother Janamma, a tyrannical woman looked after the lands. People began to resist against her atrocities. The AMS, led by Raavi Narayana Reddy, turned the movement violent with twin struggles: confiscating food grains of the landlords and fighting *vettichakiri*, bonded labour. Doddi Komuraiah, a *golla*, shepherd by caste, was shot at on 4th July, 1946 in the movement. This incident ignited the armed rebellion spreading in above 4000 villages. The Communists claim to have liberated about 3000 villages from the feudal lords, and distributed about 10,000 acres of agricultural land to the landless peasants. Around 4000 peasants lost their lives in the struggle. Though official records are not available, most of the dead happened to be sudras and dalits. In the subsequent period, the communists gave up the armed struggle, and participated in the general elections, first of its kind in the world, changing the very course of the Marxist movement in the country.

Influenced by the armed rebellion, several writers produced short stories about the movement. The Leftist movement in

Andhra Pradesh influenced the literary writing to the extent that there have been quite a few activist-writers in Telugu. Kaloji Narayana Rao's "Maname Nayam" (We are Better) depicts the life of the feudal establishment before the movement. The writer portrays two bullocks conversing about the inhuman nature of the landlords, and conclude that the animal predicament is better than that of the humans. The author describes in detail how the human beings subject the animals to cruel torture. He describes the pitiable condition of the people through one of the two bullocks. Potlapalli Rama Rao, another important writer of the early period describes in his story, "Mamullu" (Bribery) the way landlords accumulated wealth by illegally collecting revenue. This story functions as a warning to the people who were passive without offering resistance to the illegal activities of the landlords.

Vattikota Alwaru Swamy is one of the most important writers of the Telangana armed rebellion. In his story "Pariga" (The Glean), he describes how a poor man called Mallaiah is imprisoned for three months just for gleaning in the harvested fields. Alwaru Swamy's "Chinnapude" (In the Childhood) describes the popularity of the sanghams among the people. The villagers adore the leader of the sangham, who instills self-confidence in the people making them united. "Antha Aikyamaithe" (If all were United) is about how the Brahmins had to flee the villages because of the atrocities of the razakars and the landlords. However, the Brahmins were rescued by the sanghams in the villages. It is interesting that the people were united irrespective of the differences of caste, colour, creed and gender. However, it may be noted that dalits and sudras, when they are at risk, the same kind of solidarity is not reciprocated by the Brahmins and other upper castes.

Avula Pichaiah's "Itha Ginja Echi Thati Ginja Lagina Jamindar" (Landlord, who Offered a Little and Grabbed More) portrays how the poor people suffer because of their debt and the failure of the government in mitigating the problems of the people. The story also explains how the farmers become labourers in their own lands because of the perennial debt. Potlapalli Rama Rao's "Nyayam" (Justice) deals with the exploitation of the soldiers in the guise of revenue collectors. The practice of the bribery is portrayed in the story.

Kanchanapalli Chinnavenkata Rama Rao's "Meeting Mugisindi" (The Meeting Concluded) is about the exploitation of the bureaucracy in the Nizam's government. His "Cheruvu Odduna" (On the Bank of the Tank) portrays how people were united keeping aside the differences of caste and religion. The story suggests that the religious unity alone is of no use since the exploiters exist in every religion. One may understand that Raheem in "Raheem Bhai" and Lathif in "Cheruvu Odduna" never believe in religion. In fact, Raheem Bhai prefers death to joining hands with his enemy. Thus, these two stories indicate that many stories of the armed rebellion are about the unity of the people.

The story "Raheem Bhai" (My Brother, Raheem) delineates how a farmer is subjected to murder for questioning a landlord. Raheem protests against the landlord and the people around him. Suravaram Pratap Reddy's "Sangham Panthulu" (Sangam Teacher) depicts the atrocities of the police. This story is representative of the self-governed sanghams at the village level, and there was no need for police any longer. Though idealistic, the story is reformative.

Venkata Rao's "Daavath" (Party) is about the changes that took place because of the awareness on the part of the people. The revenue collectors and the employees were no longer accorded honour and respect in the same way they used to be earlier. The change was brought about by the rebellion. In "Mana Urulo Kudana" (In Our Village too?), the writer portrays the transition of the people in the villages. The story depicts incidents that resulted in the people organising themselves.

In all the stories of the period before the movement, one

understands that the awareness of the people was on the rise preparing them for an organised protest. This trend indicates that the period was preparing the people for the ensuing armed rebellion. As a result, the political movements became intensified. The Communists, writes Chandra Pulla Reddy, began to provide leadership to the Telangana movement:

> The Marxists formed different groups from 1930 to 1940 in the state of Nizam. The youngsters, who were earlier influenced by the Nationalistic movement, were attracted by the Communist ideology. Thus there was a strong desire in the cadre to work for the liberation of the working classes. (Pulla Reddy, 7)

By 1940s, the communists began their agitations in the villages decisively. They educated the people about the exploitation of the landlords. They could build a strong movement against the Deshmukhs and Jagirdars by 1944. The people demanded their lands back from the landlords. However, they realised slowly that it was not possible to get their lands legally. Therefore they decided to organise the people against the Nizam and the landlords, and grab the lands from them. Venkateswar Rao writes:

> The people could violate the law and take into their possession three thousand acres of land by 1946. They also got back the money and the grains that the landlords had collected from them as revenue. Having formed associations at village level, they rescued the people. Thus the landlords lost their control in the villages. (Venkateshwar Rao, 161)

As a consequence, the landlords attacked the people with the help of the police. The people, however, organised themselves to offer strong resistance. Chandra Pulla Reddy writes in this regard: "The Communist party proposed that the distributed lands should be retained with the people. The cases against the people must be waived. The people and the leaders arrested should be released. But the military government rejected these demands" (Pulla Reddy, 25).

The people having intensified their struggles, the movement spread into the newer areas. The union Government sent the army consisting of sixty thousand soldiers. In spite of deploying the army, the Government could not contain the armed rebellion, and it grew stronger.

Meanwhile differences among the communist leaders cropped up by 1944 regarding the issue of continuance of the armed rebellion. The Andhra Maha Sabha held separate sessions under the communist leadership. Consequently the communist party declared ceasefire of the armed rebellion in 1951. The critics of the leaders consider this decision one of the historical mistakes leading to a setback to the Leftist politics in the state.

Several short stories were written under the influence of the armed rebellion. Naveen writes in this regard: "There was no aspect of life that literature did not touch upon. Just as the armed rebellion was the axis of the movement, the land question was the axis of literature too. Stories, novels and songs were closer to the people depicting the depths of their lives" (Naveen, x). There have been above one hundred stories on the Telangana armed rebellion and twelve novels. The novels in this movement include *Muthyala Chethulu, Simha Gharjana, Prajala Manishi, Gangu, Janapadam and Sangham*, which became prominent among the cadre and activists. The writers in Telugu "have always been in tune with the changing trends in the literary prose" (Sarma, 39). In theoretical parlance, the success of the Leftist short story has to do with, what George Lukacs termed it, perspective or political commitment:

> In any work of art, perspective is of overriding importance. It determines the course and content; it draws together the threads of narration; it enables the artist to choose between the important and the superficial, the crucial and the episodic. The direction in which characters develop is determined by perspective, only those features being described which are materials to their development. The more lucid the perspective...the more economical and striking the selection. (Lukacs, 173)

Thus, the Telugu short story has drawn from the philosophy of Marxism and the Russian and the Chinese revolutions. The Indian activist-writers in several regional languages enriched the genre of short story in general and Telugu in particular. However, the Indian version of socialism has been subjected to criticism, as Sharma would view it:

> They all thought (naively, in retrospect) that an ideal society will emerge, where there will be one class with equality as the basis with the old baggage of religion and culture (described as the opium of the masses) discarded. The promised "New World" (Maro Prapancham of Sri Sri) would be under the red flag and unify the proletariat. The entire history has been recast as class conflict—between the few (rich and powerful) exploiters and the many (poor and innocent) exploited. (Sharma, 35)

Sharma is of the opinion that the Indian Leftists believed in the seemingly simple solution for establishing the utopia by the annihilation of the class enemy. He criticises that "the arm-chair version produced progressive writers forming Arasam, Virasam...etc., the fact that the original Lenin-Stalin-Mao versions only inspired bloodshed was not clearly understood by Telugu writers" (Sharma, 35).

However, it appears that Sharma is naïve in criticising the Leftist writers. Authors like Muppala Ranganayakamma immensely contributed to the formation of the Indian realist fiction. Her critique, *Ramayana Vishavriksham* is significant in deconstructing the epics and constructing the new fiction. To propose that *Ramayana* is the root cause of all evils is no small a matter keeping in view the conservative thinking of the Indians.

It may be said that the Indian communists failed to indigenise the Leftist theory to the objective social and political conditions. From the moderate to the extreme communists (ML) and their literary writings could not address seminal issues that include caste and gender.

In spite of the limitations of the class-based writing and politics, the Indian socialists, communists and Maoists played a significant role in the transformation of the feudal character of India, especially in the rural areas. In this respect, the Leftist short story in Telugu carved a niche for itself in the history of the Telugu short stories.

The limitation of the Leftist activist-writing has been that the writers valorised and celebrated the armed rebellion. The stories do not take into account the social aspect of the rebellion, and connive at the fact that the upper castes provided leadership drawing the cadre from sudras and dalits. The net effect of the movements is that the leaders at the top are safe and the cadre working at the grassroots loses their lives, which is valorised as martyrdom. The short stories of the Telangana armed rebellion are oblivious of this social realism. The second limitation of the movement as well as the corresponding short story has been that the land struggles did not benefit the sudras and dalits. When the subedars and other representatives of the Nizam had to flee the Telangana region following the Police Action, the upper caste leaders took away their lands either free of cost or at a throw away price in the panic sale. Thus, the rhetoric of the land struggles, land distribution and the slogan of land to the tiller did not benefit the sudras and dalits. The short story of the armed rebellion is silent on this aspect, for most of the writers of the period were upper castes necessarily not believing in the question of caste.

Dalits and Land

The dalit understanding of the land rights, however, is not in agreement with the claims of the Left in respect of land distribution. The dalits constitute a large number of the Leftist cadres. Among the 4000 peasants, who died in the rebellion, most of them were dalits and sudras. But the dalits hardly benefitted from the distribution of the lands. In the second phase of the Leftist movement in the seventies and eighties, the Naxalites occupied the lands of the landlords, earmarked with red flags, but hardly did the lands belong to the dalits. This aspect of dubious land distribution has been portrayed critically in the dalit fiction. A protagonist in Vemula Yellaiah's eponymous dalit novel *Kakka* addresses his landlord:

> So you are the patels and patvaris now? Did you too not work for wages? Did you not graze the horses of the Muslim lords? Did you not render services to them as their bonded labourers? When they left the place, you grabbed their lands after killing their heirs. You now boast of being patels and patvaris? (Yellaiah, 2000: 130)

Later again, he explains to the government official, who visits the village for arbitrating a dispute between the dalits and landlords:

> Was it his father alone who was a Communist? How did he become a leader without the participation of the madigas? When he hid behind the boulders, it was our men who bled while the razakars made elephants walk on them, torturing them to know the whereabouts of his father. His father neither faced nor fought the razakars. He became a leader because he hid. We don't find fault with the Telangana armed struggle; they fought seriously. But we can't get even a stretch of seven feet land for burying our dead. How did they get so much land? The entire lands of Telangana were in the name of the Nizam. When they were offered a little land, the leadership and positions in the village, the patels and doras stopped the struggle, and grabbed all the lands. Our grandparents told us all about this. (Yellaiah, 2000: 135)

Another aspect of the land rights vis-à-vis dalits is the alienation of land by the coastal Andhra peasantry. Kamma landlords, who accumulated wealth by means of green revolution, expanded their farming in the Telangana plains. Buying fertile lands in the Telangana, the coastal farmers set up, what have come to be known as 'Guntur Palle' meaning Guntur hamlets within Telangana. Yellaiah portrays the domination of the coastal farmers in Telangana.

> 'I'll tell you the tale of the fort, the tale of the Nizam. The fort was meant for keeping sentry for the village. When the thief is inside the house, of what use the sentry? The thieving upper castes of neighbouring villages forcibly entered houses. They robbed the toe-rings and pusthe of the women. They made money. The patels and doras were the agents of the Nizam, sir! Innocent people participated in the movement, trusting the leaders and not eyeing the wealth of the Nizam. The patels and doras have now become landlords, amassing vast tracts of lands by cheating us. Where did they get lands from otherwise? It is a fact that a movement was waged for Visalandhra. Are the Andhras honest people? It is true that the Nizam may have called them, but how is it that they continued to live here even after the Nizam left? We offered them lands on tenancy for feeding and training our teams in the struggles. Saline lands were left for us. They will not help us anyway. May they be damned!' (140-41)

However, this is not to reject out rightly the iconic Telangana armed rebellion, which played a significant role in questioning the authority of the landlords. But the dalit intelligentsia question that the Left lured the dalits with the promise of lands, while the struggle should have been for political power. In an interview, dalit ideologue Vemula Yellaiah states:

> It is a question of diversion from caste to land. We were diverted from fighting against the upper castes. At a time when we should have been waging struggles against untouchability, caste, political power, we were lured by the Left with the hope of getting land, and they made us a party to their so-called struggle for land. Drawing their cadre from among the innocent dalits, the Left in Andhra grew to the extent of waging armed struggles in the thirties and forties...they got lands and power. We remained where we were. It took time for dalits to realise this conspiracy, and come out of the jaws of the

> Left. Our exit from the Left was the beginning of dalit activities and writing. (Yellaiah, 2009: 337-38).

Yellaiah is critical of the claims of the Left regarding the land. For instance the slogan 'land to the tiller' benefited the tillers, who were tenants. Dalits have been rarely tenants: they have no access to land and water, and they have been only labourers and farmhands.

A typical feature of the dalits owning land is that they cannot cultivate though they own the land because of *vetti*, free labour. There have been literary representations of their inability to cultivate the lands they owned. Bhagya Reddy Verma for instance portrayed in an interesting short story, "Vetti Madiga" as early as 1932. The story deals with the subtle aspect of vetti in relation to dalits' holding of the lands. It was the turn of one madiga Malladu to render vetti to the landlord. But the same day the landlord, to whom he had to render vetti, was to harvest the paddy in his own fields. Hence madiga Malladu was in a dilemma whether to attend to the work in his own lands or to oblige the landlord. If he were to oblige Ram Reddy patel, he would have to do it at the cost of neglecting his own work; if he were not to render vetti, he would be the cause of adding fuel to the fire. He meets the patel for pleading with him to send someone else for the work. Meanwhile, the *talaari*, attendant came with raging eyes, and began to drag madiga Malladu thrashing and abusing him. The patel bangs madiga Malladu. With the confidence that madiga Malladu would not beat him back, the patel went on beating him till his hands ached. However, madiga Malladu did not protest, and fainted because of thrashing. Wounded, madiga Malladu was bed-ridden for six months, with his wife and children growing frail having nothing to eat.

Similar aspect of owning the land but not entitled to tilling is portrayed by Jupaka Subhadra in a captivating story, "Manyem." The story, which is about a Dakkali, dependent caste, portrays the social practice of alienating a section of dalits from land. Dakkali caste people live by begging the madigas narrating the family lineage of the latter. Even if the Dakkali owns land, they are not supposed to cultivate it; they have to give the land to madiga on tenancy in return to which the latter offer them grains in the harvesting season. Another instance of dalits' inability to cultivate their land because of the caste system is portrayed by Gumpula Venkateswarlu, a Begari by caste. The writer portrays a strange experience of rendering vetti at the cost of his own work. The people of Begari caste attend to cremation and other related work concerning digging graves, burying or burning the dead. Once, a death occurs in the house of a landlord by name Sitaram Reddy, who orders four of the Begaries to inform his relatives in the neighbouring villages about the death. One of them expresses his inability to do so owing to his need to attend to his work in the fields. Naganna, a begari says: "I have to till the land and sow seeds. If not today, the sowing will never take place; I don't know what to do" (Venkateswarlu, 89). But another Begari forces him to oblige the landlord as there was hardly any other option. Neglecting the work in his land, he obliges the dora.

The classic example of dalits' alienation from land is portrayed by Gogu Shyamala in her "But Why Shouldn't the Baindla Woman Ask for Her Land?" which delineates how an ordinary woman fights for her land rights. A Baindla woman, who performs by profession the role of an *erpula*, priest offering prayer to dalit goddesses, demands the dora to return her land. The dora find it difficult digest the protest of a dalit woman. Contrary to the protest of a dalit woman, is the passivity, inability and helplessness of a dalit family as portrayed by Y.B. Satyanarayana in his interesting autobiography *My Father Balaiah* (2012). Dealing with dalits' encounter with the colonial India as well as Nizam's feudal Hyderabad state, the narrative portrays as to how the Nizam gifts fifty acres of land to Narsiah as a reward to the shoes that he made and offered to the Nizam. However, Narsiah was never allowed to cultivate the land, and forty eight of fifty acres of land was grabbed by the local landlord. Narrator Satyanarayana writes:

> 'You son of a bitch, untouchable pig! How dare you present a gift to *sarkar* and receive land from him?' shouted the Dora...
>
> 'You bastard, you are an untouchable! What will you do with fifty acres of land? Do you want to become a landlord and start sitting beside me?' roared the Dora.
>
> 'No, no, Dora, how can I commit such a sin? An untouchable like me can never become a landlord. God will punish me. I will go blind. You are my lord, Dora!'
>
> The Dora calmed down at this, and looking mercifully at him, said, 'Bastard, take two acres from that gifted land and cultivate it for your family.' Turning to his clerk, he ordered, 'Go and take the rest into account as our land.'
>
> Narasiah felt relieved. He was elated at being allowed to retain the two acres. (Satyanarayana, 15)

This is an example of the nexus between caste and land. It was not uncommon that the Nizams gifted lands to the dalits. But the landlords belonging to Reddy and Velama castes denied the dalits their right to cultivate. Not stopping with the denial, the landlords grabbed the lands from the dalits. This practice of denial of right to land and right to cultivate continued from generation to generation. With the passage of sixty years of time, the landlord's son began to demand Narsiah to surrender the remaining two acres of land. When the former refused, his family had to face the Dora's wrath. Water supply to the land cut, the family members were heckled, harassed and insulted. Satyanarayana narrates:

> There was great pressure to surrender his piece of land to the Dora after the harvesting season. He was very sad that he should be losing his land after his father's death. No one in the village came out in his support since even his clansmen were of the opinion that being an untouchable, he was not supposed to hold land. (Satyanarayana, 15)

Though not precisely because of caste question, Dr B.R. Ambedkar opposed small holdings of land in his seminal essay, "Small Holdings in India and their Remedies," in which Dr Ambedkar proposed cooperative farming and industrialisation. Dr Ambedkar's opposition to small holdings is applicable to the dalits particularly because of caste and cultural problems. Conventionally, dalits are understood as the work force with or without wages.

The land reforms since the 1950's and the green revolution since the 1960's did not benefit the dalits. Dr Ambedkar therefore criticised the tiny size and the scattered and fragmented locations of the land as responsible for the uneconomical nature of farming. His criticism was based on economic principle of productivity. The small holdings and fragmented locations, he argued, raise the cost of production giving low yield, "when farming was the only occupation, to get a small piece of land was better than to have none" (Ambedkar, 480). Dr Ambedkar however suggested industrialisation as a workable remedy.

The dalits' struggles for identity and political power in Telangana had been subsumed and therefore delayed because of the Leftist struggles. The class-based struggles of the latter disguised the need for caste-based struggles, and concomitantly the social transformation. This could be one of the possible reasons for the delay in the dalits' assertion in electoral politics when compared to a state like Uttar Pradesh, where dalits could rise to the state of grabbing power. Coinciding with the identity movement in the other parts of the country, and because of the expansion of the Ambedkarite awareness, the dalits in Telangana have grown to assert themselves in the mainstream electoral politics and social transformation. Correspondingly, the dalit writing in Telangana too has come of age both in terms of using the dialect and addressing the range of themes.

References

Ambedkar, B.R. "Small Holdings in India and their Remedies." *Writings and Speeches.* Vol. 1, 1918. Print.

Gumpula Venkateswarlu, "Byagarollu." *Dalita Kathalu*, Vol. 8, ed.

Laxminarayana, Anantapuram: Rama Publications, 2000. Print.

Krishnamurthy, B.H. and Vijayasree, C. "Introduction." *Gold Nuggets: Selected Post-Independence Telugu Short Stories.* New Delhi: Sahitya Akademi, 2004. Print.

Kutumba Rao, Kodavatiganti. "Naa Story Rachana." *Sahitya Vyasalu.* Hyderabad: Viplava Rachayitala Sangham. 2001. Print.

Lukacs, George. *The Meaning of Contemporary Realism.* London: Merlin Press, 1979. Print.

Naveen, Vasireddy. *Telugu Katha 1960-85.* Hyderabad: Hyderabad Book Trust, 1991. Print.

Pandu Ranga Rao, Vakati. "Telugu Short Story: New Directions." *Indian Literature 166.* (Mar-April 1995). Print.

Pulla Reddy, Chandra. *Veera Telangana Vipulava Poratam.* Hyderabad: Vimochana Prachuranalu, 1984. Print.

Ranga Rao. "Afterword." *Classic Telugu Short Stories.* New Delhi: Penguin India, 1995. Print.

Sarma, C.R. *Landmarks: Telugu Literature.* Madras: Laxminarayana Grandhamala, 1975. Print.

Satyanarayana, Y.B. *My Father Balaiah.* New Delhi: Harper Collins, 2011. Print.

Sharma, V.V.S. "Political and Social Reality in Telugu Fiction."19/1/2012. Web.

Shyamala, Gogu. *Father may be an Elephant and Mother only a Small Basket, but….* New Delhi: Navayana Publishing, 2012.

Subhadra, Jupaka and Gogu Shyamala, ed. *Nallaregati Sallu: Madiga Upakulala Adolla Kathalku.* Hyderabad: Maisamma Sabbanda, 2006.

Sudarshanam, R.S. "Trends of Realism in the Telugu Novel." 19/1/2012. Web.

Venkateswara Rao, Devulapalli. *Bharatha Janatha Prajathantra Viplavam Karyakramam: Oka Vivarana.* Hyderabad: Proletarian Line Prachurana, 1981. Print.

Yellaiah, Vemula. "Our Exit from the Left was the Beginning of dalit Literature." in *Journal of Literature and Aesthetics*, Vol. 9, No. 1 and 2 (Jan-Dec 2009).

——. *Kakka.* Nalgonda: Gosangi Prachuranalu, 2000. Print.

8

Telugu Dalit Poetry: An Overview

Dalit poetry in Telugu, as in the other Indian languages, passed through three phases: written about, writing themselves and writing about the dependent dalit castes. Each phase, generating newer genres and styles, influenced the mainstream writing.

Written About

In the entire history of Telugu literature, dalits have never been written about positively except by the medieval mystics—Potuluri Veerabrahmam, a sudra social reformer and Yogi Vemana, a non-brahmin—both of whom questioned social evils. However, nineteenth century social reform and twentieth century nationalist poetry, though both dealt with untouchability, suffer from the limitation of silence on the religious sanctity of caste.

Mystics

Actively touring dalit and sudra streets, Potuluri Veerabrahmam and Yogi Vemana educated people on self-respect, social equality and untouchability. They became popular because of their zeal to reform and due to their simplicity in language. Their writings as well as their lives, subsequently, were subject to obliteration: Veerabrahmam, who became a cult figure, was said to have committed *sajiva rahmin*, burying oneself alive. Dalit intellectuals in the modern period say that upper caste people, unable to digest his popularity, could have buried him alive or forced him bury himself. Similarly, Vemana, who questioned rahmin hegemony, was branded insane. Their works were either made unavailable or misinterpreted. It was an Englishman, C.P. Brown (1798-1884), who edited and recorded the lost verses of Vemana. He had to depend upon local educated rahmin for tracing and recording Vemana's verses. In the process, the scribes either suppressed or misinterpreted the extant works. What is available of Vemana today can only be what escaped the eye of the rahmin and what Brown preserved.

The mystics' poetry led to a drastic change in Telugu language and literature. For the first time, untouchables became the subject of literature. Since Hinduism as a religion has been averse to reformation and modernisation, the mystics attempted reform by questioning the basis of social inequality and discrimination. Veerabrahmam, known for his *Kalagnanam*, predicting time visualised:

When everyone subordinates you

your chances of reigning the empires would be ripe

the same people who scolded you

will be cured of their stupidity

and will themselves begin to adore you.

A tradition thus started was to suffer a break in the subsequent times.

Reform

After a protracted hiatus for about five hundred years, caste and untouchability came to the fore in the nineteenth century reform by Gurajada Appa Rao (1862–1915) and Kandukuri Veeresalingam (1848-1919), who championed the concerns of upper caste women. The reform movement expanded its scope to educating people against social evils like untouchability, child marriage, bride-money, caste and religious hatred. While the mystics used song and verse, nineteenth century reformers used the short story didactically.

The reform movement however suffered the limitation of not coming to terms with the basic tenets and framework of Hinduism and the caste system. It did not continue the medieval *bhakti* tradition. Reform was also considered a reaction to dalits' conversion to Islam and Christianity.

While historiographers consider both works as benchmarks in mainstream Telugu literature, *Kanyasulkam* (1892), Gurajada Apparao's play and Veeresalingam's novel *Rajasekhara Charitam* (1880), the first Telugu novel, are silent on caste and untouchability.

Nationalist

Nationalist poetry in the subsequent period too did not question the bases of caste. Dalit struggles and their challenge to subordination were not represented in nationalist poetry. Early leaders of the nationalist movement such as Tanguturi Prakasam, Pattabhi Seetharamaiah and Burgula Ramakrishna Rao privileged transliterations/translations of Sanskrit works, undermining original Telugu, since the latter was considered the language of dalits and sudras *a la* English, which used to be considered the language of the poor during the formative years of English language. Nationalist literature did not reflect dalit and sudra life. Unnava Laxminarayana's novel, *Malapalli* (1922) and N. G. Ranga's *Harijana Nayakudu* (1933) represent this dimension. Therefore, the Gandhian agenda of 'harijan upliftment' was criticised by dalit writers like Jala Rangaswami:

You say that you are the descendants of sages

you call us brothers

you boast of following the teachings of Gandhi

nobody follows (him),

is this not injustice?

You forget the words of Mahatma Gandhi

you burn with anger at the untouchables.

The Left

Similarly, the progressive literature of the 1940s too sought to sideline socio-cultural specificities like caste, gender and ethnicity. Marxist poets, themselves upper castes, neglected caste specific exploitation. Andhra Pradesh has a long history of Leftist movements, from moderate to extreme. During the Telangana armed rebellion (1946-48), the Srikakulam peasant uprising (1957-1967) and the Naxalite movement, a large body of poetry was produced. Literary associations—Progressive and Revolutionary—iconised rahmin writers like Gurajada, Sri Sri and neglected dalit writers. For instance, in *Vaithalikulu*, an anthology of 26 modern Telugu poets of the 1930s edited by a progressive poet Muddukrishna, a noted dalit poet Jashuva was conspicuously absent. Politics was no exception: Kancha Ilaiah notes that the Congress party could nominate a dalit, Damodaram Sanjivayya as its president, but not the Indian left, which advocates the dictatorship of the proletariat.

Social reformers, nationalists and leftists did not have liberation of dalits on the agenda. As a result, the poetry of the reform, nationalist and leftist period had limited appeal. Mass appeal lay with cultural troupes like that of the Praja Natya Mandali and Jana Natya Mandali, which reached out to the masses with song and ballet. Gaddar, a dalit balladeer, who works with the left, is a phenomenon because he draws in his songs entirely from dalit language and dalit imagery. Others in this lineage include Suddala Hanmanthu, Nazar, Vangapandu, among others. The contrast between revolutionary poetry and songs has been that the former drew from Sanskrit and the epics and the latter from native Telugu and dalit life.

Writing the Self

Literary historians neglected dalit poetry written parallel to the mainstream one. Kusuma Dharmanna, for instance, wrote against caste oppression, untouchability and discrimination focusing on the Adi Andhra; Boyi Bheemanna claimed that the dalits were descendants of Arundhati and

Vashishta; Jala Rangaswami denounced the Aryan conquest that enslaved the dalits, and wrote about the glory of the pre-Aryan past; and Gurram Jashuva, who declared caste and poverty his enemies, was critical of the complaisant and self-serving poets who were unmindful of socio-economic problems:

One is a romantic poet, the other a poet with a heart of stone

one more, a poet who weeps—

Together, they console each other.

How will this Indian nation flourish?

Dalit poetry forced Telugu literature to become realistic. Deviating from the sickeningly subjective romantic poetry and the revivalist neoclassical poetry, dalit poetry created a new literary space.

In the post-Independence period, complaisant mainstream writers were bombarded by six *Digambara Kavulu*, (naked poets) providing the much-needed jolt to Telugu literature by re-linking literature to society. They dedicated their 1968 anthology to a dalit boy Kanchikarla Kotesh, who was burnt alive by the upper castes accusing him of theft. This incident can be considered the forerunner of the identity movements—dalit, feminist and *adivasi,* in times to come.

'Dalit Mahasabha,' the first organised modern dalit movement, launched by poet-activist Kathi Padma Rao and civil rights champion Bojja Tarakam in 1985, began to fight the atrocities at Karamchedu, Neerukonda, Thimma Samudram, Chundur, Vempenta and Cherlapally. Since then, young dalits began to produce a powerful body of poetry. In 1995, the first anthology of Telugu dalit poetry, *Chikkanavutunna Paata* (thickening song) was edited by G. Laxminarsaiah and Tripuraneni Srinivas, followed by *Padunekkina Paata* (sharpened song, 1996) edited by G. Laxminarsaiah. Both anthologies, though not exclusively dalit, are concerted efforts to foreground dalit ethos, angst, protest, heritage, myth and an alternative vision. Some dalit poets in the anthologies emerged with new voices, giving a direction to young and emerging dalit poets, who later on brought out a number of anthologies and little magazines, which served as platforms for new debates.

Writing About

The malas, being relatively more developed because of fertile lands, irrigation facilities, exposure to British rule, missionary education, medical services and the church, are politically, economically and otherwise, stronger. Malas treat madigas as untouchable, and both of them treat their dependent castes as untouchables. This *inter se* untouchability has become the subject of poetry as a result of the identity movement spearheaded by the Dandora movement, championing the cause of proportionate access to reservation benefits, as a poet questions the notion of supremacy within dalits:

When the meal is intended for both of us

how is it that I am prevented from eating it?

And another poet questions the sanctity accorded to divisiveness by religion:

the saffron tree that

separates the eyebrows of

the dalit mother.

The movement, launched for equity within dalits, resulted in foregrounding the identity question. It led to reclamation of identity and self-respect with the suffixing of 'madiga' to their names. A term, hitherto considered filthy, became a symbol of identity and self-respect. This is a symbolic achievement of the Dandora movement. Influenced by the movement, seasoned poets like Kolakaluri Enoch, Yendluri Sudhakar and young poets like Vemula Yellaiah, Nagappagari Sunderraju, among several others, earned respectability for what was once despised as obscene and trash. They wrote about madiga identity in dalit language and dialect, hitherto considered unfit for poetry.

Similarly, madiga women writers like Gogu Shyamala, Jupaka Subhadra, Jajula Gowri and others have been writing about the dual oppression. Besides, they have been writing about the dependent dalit castes like dekkali, chindu, begari, among others. An important feature of dalit feminist writing is that they were not written about by their upper caste counterparts, but themselves are writing about their counterparts among subordinate dalits. This is the unique feature of dalit feminist writers in Telugu.

The dependant castes are yet to write themselves: they still need to grow from being written about to writing themselves. Telugu dalit poetry, in this respect, has a long way to go. When dalit poetry shows the tendency of repeating itself, emergence of writers from below enlivens it with newer genres, styles and force. This happened in the 2000s with the emergence of madigas, followed by madiga women writers. Similarly a possible emergence of writers from the dependent dalit castes in times to come is likely to enrich dalit poetry in far more innovative ways. The achievement of dalit poetry has thus been reclaiming dalitness in all its forms and influencing and shaping the mainstream poetry, especially in privileging the individual experiences, asserting identity and using a simple language.

This anthology is an attempt at presenting before the readers the oeuvre of the dalit poetry in Telugu. Seventy three selections in all, drawn from thirty nine poets of the first generation to the latest, presents a wide variety of times, themes, ideologies, styles and concerns. Representing a period of above hundred years, the poems reflect the transition and development of dalit poetry as a genre in Telugu. Beginning from protest and assertion, the writings went on to be mature to seek alternatives in the cultural resources of dalits drawn from dalit deities, rituals, rites, dalit theatre, dialect and dalit language. While the translator took every care to overcome the burden of monotony of 'one-man's translations,' it is hoped that the readers will recreate in their reading the dalit ethos—travails, tribulations, challenges and aesthetics.

Profiles of Telugu Dalit Poets

Gurram Jashuva

Jashuva (1895-1971), who worked in an elementary school, was recognised as the voice of the depressed castes, and received public acclaim and literary honour. Born of a *golla*, shepherd father and madiga mother, he was raised in the Christian tradition, which excommunicated him for drawing from Hinduism in his writings. Though graduated with *ubhaya bhasha pravina,* scholar of Telugu and Sanskrit, Jashuva was insulted by the upper castes by excluding him from the social space and the contemporary anthologies. Known for strict metre with progressive thought, he authored 22 creative works, and was a recipient of Padma Vibhushan, honorary doctorate, Sahitya Akademy award and was nominated to the Legislative Council of AP. Modeled after Kalidasa's *Meghasandesham*, his *Gabbilam*, a long poem, describes a message sent by a dalit to the god through a bat.

Kusuma Dharmanna

A staunch critic of Gandhi and Hinduism, Dharmanna (1898-1948) presided over the *Adi-Andhra* (aboriginal) conferences. A farmer, activist-writer and orator, he ran a periodical, *Jayabheri,* to propagate Dr Ambedkar's ideology. He encouraged dalits to convert to Islam. He authored four important works and the present song written in 1921, which aroused the youth, was the dalit reply to "We Decry this European Supremacy" by a nationalist caste-Hindu writer, Garimella Satyanarayana. Dalits widely believe that Dharmanna's song was written prior to Garimella's.

Boyi Bhimanna

Boyi Bhimanna (1911-2005) was born in East Godavari district. He was a writer, freedom fighter, teacher, journalist and a member of Legislative Council. He was influenced by the teachings of Mahatma Gandhi and Dr B. R. Ambedkar, and on the latter, he brought out four books in different genres and translated *The Annihilation of Caste* first time into Telugu. He was known for advocating unity between malas and madigas and for propounding the theory of dalits as the early Aryans. A director of the A.P. translation division and winner of 'Padmasri,' 'Padma Bhushan,' an honorary doctorate and Akademy award, he authored 70 books, including an English collection, *Seventh Season*. His play *Paleru* inspired many dalits to give up farmhand work and seek education and jobs. The following selections are from his Akademy Award winning anthology, *Gudiselu Kalipotunnayi.*

Sivasagar

Sivasagar (Kambhampati Gnana Satyamurthy, 1928-2012) started off his career as a teacher, and was a founder member of the Peoples War (ML). He left the party, accusing it of being casteist. Known for his anthology, *Udyamam Nelabaaludu*, Sivasagar, the activist-writer penned many books, articles and poems, and is considered a trendsetter in both revolutionary and dalit poetry. As a poet, he left an indelible mark both on the revolutionary poetry in the beginning and dalit poetry in the last two decades. His style is cryptic and imagery drawn from rural and dalit life.

Kolakaluri Enoch

Born in Guntur district of coastal Andhra, Kolakaluri Enoch (1939-) has been a distinguished professor of poetry, critic, administrator and statesman. A seasoned writer credited with writing in all the genres, he has published four anthologies of poetry, seven anthologies of short stories and 14 novels and plays. He is one of the early writers to have asserted dalit identity, and is known for writing on other than dalit theme too. Prof Enoch served as the vice-chancellor of Sri Venkateshwara University, Tirupathi, and received, among several others, the Best Teacher and Akademy awards.

Boya Jangaiah

Boya Jangaiah (b.1942) was born in a small village in Nalgonda district of the Telangana region. He has published two novels, *Jathara* and *Jagadam*, two anthologies of short stories besides plays and *Boya Kavithalu*, an anthology of his poetry. One of the early Telugu dalit writers, he has been a recipient of several awards including the one by Telugu University.

G.R. Kurme

Born in Adilabad district, Ganga Ram Kurme (b.1947) was one of the founder members of 'Darakame,' (Forum for dalit writers, artists, intellectuals) founded in 1992 which provided platform to the dalit writers for rallying support and generating debates on various issues concerning dalit discourses—social, political and literary. A recipient of important awards, he has published several anthologies and *Dammapatham*, a long poem on Lord Buddha, is significant among them. Kurme is known for brevity and apt imagery in his poetry.

Gaddar

Gaddar (Gummadi Vittal Rao, b. 1949), a revolutionary balladeer and vocal Naxalite activist, gave up engineering education and a job in a bank, to form a cultural troop, 'Jana Natya Mandali,' a frontal organisation of the then Peoples War (ML) in order to disseminate cultural revolution. Living under police repression, Gaddar survived an attempt on his life. He has earned respectability for the folk art forms with several young balladeers imitating him, shirtless, donning a coarse rug, and a dhoti as a shepherd. A staunch supporter of the Telangana movement, Gaddar is known for the stage performances mixed with song and speech arousing the youth to action, his songs on the martyrs are especially moving and thought provoking.

Kathi Padma Rao

Padma Rao (b. 1953) taught Sanskrit and subsequently became a full-time activist. A founder of 'Dalit Mahasabha,' he fought against atrocities in Karamchedu, Tsundur and other places. A prominent dalit activist, thinker, poet and critic, he has forty six publications to his credit, including ten anthologies of poetry. Received Honorary Doctorate from Acharya Nagarjuna University in recognisition of his contribution to Dalit literature and social justice for the downtrodden in August 2007. The awards he received include Pratibha Award, Boyi Bhimanna

Trust Award, Potti Sri Ramulu Telugu University Award, Sahitya Puraskaram, Avantsa Soma Sunder Sahiti trust Award, Dr C. Narayana Reddy Sahiti Award and Ambedkar Award. Padma Rao is known for his fierce speeches supported by sound argument.

Damera Ramulu

Damera Ramulu (b. 1954) was born in Shayampet, Warangal district of the Telangana region. He completed MD in general medicine at Kakatiya Medical College, Warangal and runs a nursing home in Nirmal. An activist in the Radical Students Union when he was a medical student, Ramulu pursues his literary interest and published three anthologies of poetry, *Chorus*, *Nethuti Vennela* and *Jayahe Telangana*.

Shikhamani

Shikhamani (Karri Sanjeeva Rao, 1957-), born in Yanam, Puducheri, is a voluminous writer having eight collections of poetry and four critical works to his credit. *Muvvala Cheti Karra* and *Silakkoyya* are his important poetry collections, besides which he recently edited *Amma* (Mother), featuring poems on theme of mother. As a critic of Telugu literature, he has written extensively. Having received several state and national awards, he teaches at P.S. Telugu University, Hyderabad.

Tullimalli Wilson Sudhakar

Tullimalli Wilson Sudhakar (b. 1957), who hails from coastal Andhra, began as a journalist and presently works with Indiatourism. A double postgraduate, he published *Dalita Vyakaranam*, an anthology of poetry, and has been a winner of several awards. He has travelled about twenty five countries as a part of his profession. Sudhakar, who is planning his second collection of poems, writes exclusively on dalit themes, topical in nature reacting to the contemporary incidents.

Yendluri Sudhakar

Yendluri Sudhakar (b. 1959), son of migrants from Maharashtra is a poet and short story writer. He has published four anthologies of poetry of which ***Darky: A Bilingual***

Anthology of Poems 1985-2002 **received wide acclaim.** Though known as a poet, his prose work, *Malle Moggala Godudu* (1999) is remarkable for employing dalit language and asserting madiga identity. He is the Dean at P.S. Telugu University. Sudhakar's contribution to dalit writing in Telugu lies in re-locating dalit identity in his prose and poems.

Jajula Gowri

Born in Secunderabad, Jajula Gowri (1963-) published *Mannu Buvva* (mud-rice), an anthology of short stories. Gowri, known for her prose, occasionally writes poetry, and her preference to write on the theme of draught, earned the epithet, 'Matti Rachayitri,' mud-writer.

Satish Chandar

Satish Chandar (1958-), born in Narsapur, is a post graduate in commerce worked in the print media in different capacities. He has authored fifteen books in different genres of which *Panchama Vedam* is most acclaimed. He has been a recipient of awards in literature and journalism, which he pursues as a profession and continues to write poetry on contemporary issues.

Jupaka Subhadra

Subhadra (1963-) completed her masters in Telugu literature and took up a job at the Secretariat in Hyderabad. An activist and feminist, she writes about her experiences taking active part in social and trade union activities. *Ayyayyo Dammakka* is her collection of poetry. As a dalit activist, she participates in protest movements and contributes to the concept of dalit feminism.

Paidi Tereshbabu

Born in Ongole district, Paidi Tereshbabu (b. 1963) works as a senior grade announcer in All India Radio, Hyderabad. A voluminous writer, he has published three anthologies of poetry and won several awards. Tereshbabu wrote poetry on various aspects of dalit life with a pungent criticism of Hinduism.

Madduri Nageshbabu

Madduri Nageshbabu (1964-2005) was one of the most promising dalit writers in whose premature death Telugu dalit literature lost an activist and a talented writer. Having begun his career in the All India Radio, he published seven anthologies of poetry, four long poems and several essays. Nageshbabu belongs to that generation of writers and activists, who were uncompromising and bitter critics of caste.

Kalekuri Prasad

Kalekuri Prasad (b.1964) is a poet, essayist, columnist and translator. His prose works interpreting socio-political aspects of dalit life are considered original and insightful. One of very few English knowing dalit writers, Prasad produced writings with original insights setting a model to young and budding dalit writers.

Banna Ilaiah

Banna Ilaiah (b. 1964), a critic, poet and a professor at Kakatiya University, Warangal, was born Elguru village in Warangal district. He published two anthologies of poetry *Rahasya Chitram* and *Fire Spark*, six critical works, and has bagged several awards. Known for convincing public speeches, Prof Ilaiah published critical works on varied themes of Telugu literature.

Nagappagari Sunder Raju

Sunder Raju (1965-2000?), born in Kurnool district of Rayalaseema region is one of the early dalit intellectuals to have generated dalit discourses on the university campuses when the class-based discourses were still considered the order of the day. He brought out *Gunde Dappu*, *Chandala Chatimpu*, *Mavuri Maisamma*, *Madigodu* and founded 'Madiga Sahitya Vedika,' a forum for madiga literature. In his untimely death, Telugu dalit writing lost a committed organiser, organic thinker and a shrewd activist.

Ravinuthala Prema Kishore

Prema Kishore (b.1965), born in a village in Prakasham district authored eight plays and twelve one-act plays besides two anthologies, *Gundedaruvu* and *Naluguramavudam*. A postgraduate in history and winner of several awards, he works in the Board of Secondary School Certificate, Hyderabad.

Koyi Koteshwar Rao

A doctorate, Koteswar Rao (b.1968) was born in Prakasham district, and teaches Telugu. Though belongs to the coastal Andhra Pradesh, he published *Kavadi Kundalu* in support of the movement for separate Telangana. He is now co-editing Telugu dalit literature for Sahitya Akademy, New Delhi. Koteswar Rao is known for the skills of public speech with incisive criticism of the oppressive system.

M.M. Vinodini

M.M. Vinodini (b.1969) was born in Guntur of the coastal Andhra Pradesh. A doctorate in Telugu, she teaches at Yogi Vemana University, Cudapa. She considers herself a writer when she began to write her experiences as a dalit Christian. Popular for her much anthologised short story 'Maria,' and a dalit play, *Thurst*, which has been brought out by Oxford University Press, India. Besides writing short stories and poetry, Vinodini writes on pedagogy and women writing from dalit perspective. A powerful orator, she speaks on dalit literature quite thought provokingly.

Gogu Shyamala

Gogu Shyamala (b. 1969), a writer, critic and activist, edited *Nallapoddu*, dalit women writing, co-edited madiga women's short stories, authored a biography of the first dalit woman minister and published with Navayana her stories in English translation. A co-editor of Telugu dalit writing forthcoming with OUP India, she works with Anveshi, a Hyderabad-based women's collective. Basically a prose writer, Shyamala penned dalit poetry occasionally.

Gundedappu Kanakaiah

Born in a village in Karimnagar district, Kanakaiah (b. 1969), along with eleven other students in the University of Hyderabad, brought out *Gundedappu* (hearty drumbeat, 1997), first anthology to have come from a university in response to

Manifesto, a left-based dalit anthology. He published ten anthologies of poetry and short stories.

Challapalli Swaruparani

Swaruparani (b. 1970) Teaches Buddhist studies at Acharya Nagarjuna University, Guntur. As a poet, Swaruparani published *Mankenapuvu*, a collection of her poetry and authored several scholarly articles on themes like oral tradition, tribals and dalit women. Her poetry is characteristic of dalit feminism.

J. Goutham

Goutham (b. 1970), who was earlier a Marxist, became a dalit activist and writer. Having several dalit poems to his credit, Goutham takes active part in dalit struggles. He had launched 'Madiga Mahajana Poratasamithi,' a socio-political outfit.

Chitram Prasad

Chitram Prasad (b. 1971) belongs to Nalgonda district of the Telangana region. Having to his credit several dalit poems and a short story, Prasad works as a post master in his village.

G.V. Ratnakar

An academic, translator and poet, Ratnakar (b. 1972), who was born in Prakasham district, teaches Hindi in Moulana Azad National Urdu University, Hyderabad. He authored four books, translated several works into Telugu, including Omprakash Valmiki's *Joothan* and Dr Ambedkar's writings.

Yedla Peter Paul

Peter Paul (b. 1972), born in Guntur district, published an anthology of poetry and he works in the agricultural department. He prefers to write poetry on contemporary issued concerning dalits.

Vemula Yellaiah

Vemula Yellaiah (b.1973), born in Warangal district, has published two dalit novels, *Kakka* (2000), the English version being brought out by Navayana and *Siddi* (2004) besides several dalit poems. Pursuing his Ph.D and working as a project fellow in the University of Hyderabad, he is known for using dalit language and Telangana dialect.

Darla Venkateshwar Rao

Darla Venkateshwar Rao (b. 1973), an academic, critic and poet, was born in East Godavari district. He has authored twelve books, both creative and critical and teaches Telugu at University of Hyderabad.

Varre Rani

Varre Rani (1973-2001), who lost her parents in the cyclone, married a rahmin, who deserted her on knowing about her heart ailment. A sense of being an orphan and deserted by one who she had loved haunted her till she breathed her last.

Ponnala Balaia

Ponnala Balaia (b. 1973) was born in Arepalle, an interior village in Karimnagar district. He has published two anthologies of his poetry, besides some short stories. He teaches Hindi in a government school.

Kadire Krishna

Kadire Krishna (b. 1975), born in Nalgonda district of the Telangana region, has published an anthology of poetry and a novel. He is the president of Rashtriya Mulnivasi Sangh, AP branch and president of Bahujan Liberation Movement, AP.

Taidala Anjaiah

Anjaiah (b. 1975), born in an interior village in Karimnagar district, published *Punasa*, an anthology of his poems. He also published a few short stories. A trained teacher in mathematics, he works in a government school.

Inala Saidulu

Inala Saidulu (b. 1979), born in an interior village in Khammam district, published *Vathava Mavuriki,* a poetry anthology and edited *Swetchakosam*, an anthology of his essays, besides writing review articles and essays. A double post graduate, Saidulu teaches in a government school.

9

Gendering Caste: Emergence of Dalit Feminism

Feminism, as a concerted theory and movement, is Western in origin. There had, however been an indigenous tradition of the struggles for women's emancipation, which may be discussed under three categories: two of them being exclusivist and influenced by the West, one is inclusivist and indigenous. The pre-Independence women's reformative movement advocating widow re-marriages and against the practice of child marriages was confined to the upper castes. This movement excluded dalit and sudra women; widow re-marriages, however were common among sudra and dalit women. The post-Independence feminist movement has been by and for the liberation of the social elites, which is once again exclusivist. Led by the educated, it has been silent on dalit women's subordination by upper castes. Both the strands attempted at objectification writing off the specificities of women's subordination. The objectification, however, is a strategy of the oppressive ideology predicated on silencing the voices of identity. Dalit women, for example, articulate differently focusing their sexuality, political awareness, self-assertion, experience of profession, violence, and suffering within the community. The objectification silences these specificities. Dalit feminists, by articulating these concerns, question the philosophical and religious foundations of the Indian patriarchy, which the mainstream movements were silent on. This essay seeks to examine the historical background to the revival of dalit feminism, which is a part of the larger identity struggles taking place in India.

Modern feminist movement in India was not against the oppressive structures of power and it did not question the tenets laid down by Manu, Kautilya and Vatsayana, the founders of Indian patriarchy. The former two envisioned the subordinated status to women, and evolved the forms of punishing the subversive women. Vatsayana considered the women as mere sex objects amounting to commodification of women foreseeing the cultural capitalism in the twentieth century. The three of them denied social and political rights to women. Sanctified by Hinduism, the status of women remains in spirit the way the founders of Hindu patriarchy envisaged it to be.

The Cultural Revolt

In contrast to the status of the mainstream women, Lord Buddha preached for the equality of women in all the spheres. Buddha, according to Kancha Ilaiah, can be credited with five significant achievements: recognition of the political right of women to join the sangha; forcing the sangha to recognise women's right to be leaders; allowing women develop their personality and individuality independent of any male support; breaking the myth of family and the importance of producing male children to attain salvation; and recognition of the need for women's education and political initiative (Ialaiah, 184). The fact that Lord Buddha allowed his wife Yashodhara and mother Maha Prajapathi as his disciples is evidence enough to his vision of gender equality, which in the twentieth century was to become a political slogan. Continuing Buddha's tradition of gender equality, the mystics (Bhakti saints) fought against the Hindu orthodox practices. Their attempts at the liberation of women may be considered the cultural revolt. Though the mystics hail from different social backgrounds, their social agenda had been against the brahminical male hegemony. The impetus for their cultural revolt was in fact necessitated by the Muslim invasions, conversions and pathetic living conditions of sudras and dalits. However, the mystics broadened their agenda and questioned all forms of social subordination. Emphasising on the spiritual equality and social justice, they were equally concerned with the gender inequality in particular. Therefore they protested against the subordination of women.

An interesting aspect of the mystics' movement for the gender equality had been that the women took active part in the mystics' activities along with their men. The best example is Mirabai, a Rajasthani Rajput princess, known for her hymns in Hindi, who became a disciple of Ravidas, an untouchable saint. Accepting a guru from dalit background by a Rajput princess was a rebellion against the casteism and patriarchy of the medieval period. Another branch of the mystics' movement was the Virashaiva movement in Karnataka. A counterpart of the Bhakti movement, known for the combination of egalitarianism and spiritual excellence, the Virashaivism, explains Brajranjan Mani (166), had a strong presence of women in the movement. Many female ascetics like Akka Mahadevi and Muktayakka were part of Virashaivism in the pathbreaking work. The Virashaivism was critical of the brahminical legitimation of female subordination. The movement built a new version of the man-woman relationship. The women mystics used to assert themselves when they were not treated on par with men mystics. This aspect is unimaginable even in the contemporary situation. Other women mystics like Muktabai, Bahinabai, Soyarabai, Kannopatra and Janabai, among others, questioned the gender discrimination. A modernist aspect of the mystics' movement for gender equality had been that they gave equal importance to the all round development of women, besides gender equality.

De-Gendering through Education

The philosophy of Lord Buddha and the movements led by the mystics influenced Mahatma Jotibha Phule (1827–1890) and Babasaheb Ambedkar (1891-1956), the architects of gender politics. Phule was the first activist thinker to have launched a movement in India for the liberation of sudras, dalits and women. Considered the ideological and political founder of the socio-gender equality, he foresaw Michael Foucault (1926-1984), who later on theorised knowledge-power equation (Mani, 251). Phule knew that exclusion of women from knowledge was the main cause of women's subordination. He considered education as a vital means of women's liberation. As a part of his gender praxis, Phule first educated his wife, Savitribai (1831-1897). Together, they established eighteen schools during 1848-1852 and a separate school for dalit girls as early as 1848. By doing so, Phule adopted a radical approach to gender inequality in the mid-nineteenth century.

The missionary education during the colonial period gave opportunity to dalit and sudra women. Phule's efforts coupled with the missionary education resulted in the women's involvement in fighting against the evil practices among dalits. Meenakshi Moon and Urmila Pawar write: "Women actively involved in the early untouchable liberation movement and liberated many women out of the *devadasi* profession and found husbands for them as early as 1908" (Zelliot, 205). In Tamil Nadu, the self-respect movement led by Periyar E Ramaswamy Naicker espoused revolutionary views on marriage. His struggles against caste and gender inequality laid foundation to the plank of social equality.

Following the legacy of Buddha, Phule and other predecessors of gender movement, B.R. Ambedkar intellectualised gender equality as a part of his larger mission of social equality. He was instrumental to have interpreted caste and patriarchy as the twin sources of social inequality in general and gender inequality in particular. Ambedkar's introduction of the Hindu Code Bill in 1951 is an example of his vision of social security for women. The Hindu patriarchy, however did not allow the Bill to be passed. In Mahad Satyagraha of 1928, Nasik Satyagraha to enter the Kalaram temple (1930–35), hundreds of women held meetings to enlist support to Dr Ambedkar's declaration to convert to Buddhism. The burning of the *Manusmriti* by Dr Ambedkar in 1927 was a symbolic gesture as it denied basic human rights to women.

Phule, Periyar and Ambedkar were all non-brahmin political leaders who questioned the values of the upper-caste-dominated independence movement. All of them were much concerned with gender, and underlined the links between caste oppression and the oppression of women. The three of them, whose broader goal was social equality, perceived that social equality was possible only with gender equality.

Dalit Women Writing

Dalit women literature had been subjected to obliteration. Susie Tharu and Lalita's twin volumes of *Women Writing in India*, though a radical critique of the patriarchy, cannot be said to have represented dalit women writing. The anthologies mostly focus on the writings of the upper caste women before the late 1800s. The editors might not have considered caste as a criterion for selections, and in this sense, the anthologies suffer a limitation. The due literary space however is now being filled by the dalit anthologizers. *Nalla Poddu*, an anthology that retrieved dalit women writing in Telugu, and similar attempts in other languages only will hold testimony to the richness of dalit women writing in the early period.

In the modern period, literacy, social awareness, political awakening and identity movements resulted in a spurt of writing by dalit women in regional languages. The English publication of dalit writing is governed by the market abroad. The political correctness on the part of translators, editors, publishers and the elite academia made it possible that a large body of dalit women writing is published in English, and the same has become part of the highbrow academics.

The contemporary dalit women writers include, Urmila Pawar, Jyoti Langewar, Hira Bansode, Surekha Bhagat, Pradnya Lokhande, Mina Gajbhiye, Baby Kamble, Shantabai Kamble in Marathi; Gogu Syamala (an anthology forthcoming from Navayana), Jupaka Subadra, Jajula Gowri, M.M. Vinodini and Challapalli Swarooparani in Telugu; Siva Kami, Bama and Veeramma in Tamil. There are several others whose works are yet to appear in English translations. Accounting for the emergence of dalit feminist literature, Challapalli Swarooparani writes, "Dalits put to creative use the gains of social and literary movements. There are of course common issues that bind dalit men and women, like untouchability and caste oppression. But women also suffer from patriarchal oppression" (Swaroopa Rani, 21).

Dalit women use literature as a weapon to challenge the mainstream women writing, and the autobiography is found suitable to write the women's experiences. The most acclaimed autobiographies include, Bama's *Karruku* (2004), Viramma Josiane Racine's *Viramma: Life of a Dalit* (1997) in Tamil, Urmila Pawar's *The Weave of Life* (2009) and Baby Kamble's *The Prisons we Broke* (2008) in Marathi. These publications and many more in publishers' pipeline in the next few years, supported by sound theory, point to challenging the elite feminism, and the emergence of dalit feminism.

References

Ilaiah, Kancha, *God as Political Philosopher: Buddha's Challenge to Brahmanism*, Kolkata: Samya, 2004. Print.

Mani, Braj Ranjan. *Debrahmanishing History: Dominance and Resistance in Indian Society*. New Delhi: Manohar, 2005. Print.

Swaroopa Rani, Challapalli. "Dalit Women's Writing in Telugu." in *Economic and Political Weekly*, April 25, 1998, 21. Print.

Zelliot, Eleanor. "Dr Ambedkar and the Empowerment of Women." *Gender and Caste: Issues in Contemporary Indian Feminism*, Ed Anupama Rao, New Delhi: Kali for Women, 2006. Print.

10

A Reading of Two Feminist Poems: An Anti-Generic Critique

Generic Feminism

One of the offshoots of the self-respect movements, started in the early eighties, has been to question the epistemological notions of liberationist ideologies. The investigations of the origin and nature of the ideologies suffer from generic categorisation of the subjects. Feminism, for example, is essentially based on patriarchy as the agency of gendering. Feminist movements and scholarship in the beginnings did not take into account the race as a source of discrimination and subordination of black women. Similarly the Indian feminists did not take into account religion and caste as the sources of the Indian patriarchy, let alone language and region, the other gendering agencies. The discourses of the European feminism as well as the Indian feminism, which revolve round the patriarchy, paid no attention to the social agencies that subordinate the other gendered women.

Through generic categorisation, caste, language, region and religion are obliterated. The binaries like upper caste women and their lower caste counterparts; the educated women and their illiterate counterparts; the women from developed region and their counterparts from backward region—are posited against each other culturally and socially. In each of the gendering agencies, the former (social elites) subordinate the latter, though both belong to the same gender. The former consider the patriarchy as the source of women's subordination. The ideological configuration of, what has now emerged as, dalit feminism, partially addresses the neglected agencies of gendering. Language and region vis-à-vis gender are yet to be problematised. This paper seeks to frame the other gendering agencies—caste, language, region—by using two Telugu poems as sites of reference: Jayaprabha's much celebrated *"Paitani Tagaleyyali* (Burn this Sari, 1988) and Jupaka Subhadra's *"Kongu Naabochemiida Kaavalunde Bonthapeggaadu* (No Watchdog at my Bosom, 2007).

Emergence of Dalit Feminism

A recapitulation of the emergence of dalit feminist thought helps problematise the elite feminism and dalit feminism that the two poems represent respectively.

The typical problems that the dalit women confront, when compared to those of the elite women or the dalit men, have been debated in the social forums. The elite feminists in the erstwhile Andhra Pradesh formed a social forum, besides several others earlier, by name *Manalo Manam* (among ourselves) as a broad forum apparently encompassing the women from a cross-section of women, including the dalits. As a symbolic gesture, a dalit has been incorporated into its executive. But the forum and its agenda has quickly become the subject of criticism by the dalit women on the grounds that it has no agenda for the liberation of dalit women; the forum is silent on the question of the oppression of dalit women by the upper caste women. This led to the floating of a parallel forum, *Maalo Memu* (we are ourselves). The dalit women activists and writers have been actively engaged in framing the issues concerning dalit women as essentially different from those of the elite women both in the debates and literary anthologies.

Dalit women brought out an anthology, *Nallapoddu* (dark sunrise) in 2004 tracing the tradition of dalit women writing as far back as 1921. This anthology could be considered a dalit response to *Neelimeghalu*, an anthology by elite feminists. Considering that *Nallapoddu* suffered from limitations: that it represents mala as well as coastal writers, another anthology, *Nallaregati Saallu* (furrows of black soil), stories on madiga and its sub-castes, was published in 2006. The dalit women intelligentsia in the last decade contributed to the emergence of dalit feminism offering sharp critique of the exclusivist, elite feminism. Jupaka Subhadra, Gogu Shyamala, Jajula Gowri, M.M. Vinodini, Challapalli Swarupa Rani, Sujatha Gidla, among others, have produced a considerable body of writing. Besides the literary genres like short story, poetry and personal/family narratives, a great deal of media-based debate on feminism has been taking place. The dalit writing and debates by women is sharp and more focused than the writings of their men counterparts: "the poetry by dalit women writing [sic] from the dalit women's perspective and based on their experiences as dalit women is far more powerful and has a far greater impact than the poetry of dalit male poets or upper caste women poets. Dalit women's issues have less in common with dalit men's issues than with those of the upper caste women (Swaroopa Rani, 21). The dalit women writing, thus, represent the concerns that are unique to themselves.

One of the main contentions of the dalit women has been regarding the silence of the elite feminists on the issue of caste as a gendering agency. The first ever anthology of women writing, Tripuraneni Srinivas' *Gurichoosi Pade Paata* (singing with aimed target), 1990 and *Manaku Teliyani Manacharitra (We were Making History)*, 1986, life Stories of women in the Telangana People's Struggle. *Neelimeghalu* (blue clouds), 1993, edited by Volga carried only a dalit and a Muslim minority poet among thirty odd poets (amounting to mere three poems out of a total of ninety). A recent anthology, *Mudra: Vanithala Kavithalu* (2001) edited by Subhadra Devi and Bhargavi Rao has a hundred poems by women covering from the fifteenth century to the present, which also neglected dalit representation.

The anthologies, associations and media debates of the elite feminists point to two important trends: that their concern is primarily the family, de-mystification of motherhood and sexuality; and that they neglected dalit women's writings. *Neelimeghalu,* especially generated considerable amount of debate on the question of framing the gendering. Most of the poems explicitly deal with family, body and sexuality. In a different context, however, women's body and sexuality was described in what is known as *sringara*, sensuous writing by men. When women chose to write, it attracted criticism. S.V. Rama Rao, for example, criticised feminist poetry on the grounds that the anthology does not represent "all the women; it reflects only the desires of the urban, bigheaded rich young girls. It does not represent the economic, social and political exploitation." He further attacked the poetry as the one dealing with urine, menses, bleeding" (in *Neelimeghalu*, 213). The mainstream feminism has sought to challenge "the family, the authority-based relationships between men and women and the patriarchal structure that hides the male dominance which attributes holiness to motherhood" (Shyamala, 15).

Dalit women's writing, contrarily, mark a shift from the concerns of the elite feminists. Instead of family, de-mystification of motherhood and sexuality, the dalit women focus on caste-based patriarchy. The shift is from family and body to the caste-based patriarchy: "There have been very few dalit poems that discuss the theme of the family...the preoccupation with family is more of an upper-caste, middle-class phenomenon that does not affect most dalit women, who belong to lower classes and castes (Sridhar, 239). Dalit women writing marks a departure from the elite feminists in regard to family and women. The following section examines the select poems marking the shift in the feminist issues.

Sari-end

The *sari*-end, being an important part of the traditional Indian women's attire, the poets' choice of the *sari* as the subject is significant, for their poems provide insights to feminists' reaction to the tradition. This section examines the poems focusing on why Jayaprabha rejects the *sari* while Subhadra does not.

The first poem, "*Paitani Tagileyyali*" (paita, here after) by Jayaprabha is representative of the elite nature of the *sari*. Symbolically, it stands for the body, which is the main concern of the elite feminists. They claim their right over their body:

[sari-end] hypnotises me

telling me, 'You,

are a woman,

makes me forget I'm human.

Covers both my shoulders

with my own hands

and flutters announcing, 'See, see

this woman! She's chaste.'

I feel like screaming, 'No, no,

I'm not,'

but my throat does not open.

I'm defeated by this sari.

Paita/sari for the social elites is a burden. The poet finds fault with the sari, which is bequeathed by the tradition. The urban elite women practice double standards with regard to tradition: they are traditional at home and modern outside the home. In respect of celebrations, rituals and other aspects of culture, the urban and upper caste women scrupulously follow the tradition. Outside the family, they reject the tradition and sound/appear modern. By extension, this applies to sari too:

It pulls me in like quicksand,

it thrown me down

like a whirlwind.

It is the blame

generations have laid upon me,

the unseen patriarchal hand.

This sari is the white

shroud on the corpse

that's me in this culture

of loot and plunder.

Sari became revealingly ornamental. Popular notion about the sari as the attire is that it is the sexiest of all the attire. The roots of the sari may be traced in the Hindu notion of women and Vatsyayana's *Kamasutra.* The feminist poets, however, criticise the form without finding fault with the essence. The poet's objection to the sari is not because of it causes inconvenience in the physical movement of women; not because it does not cover the body providing protection from unfavourable atmosphere, which men's attire does. The pants and full sleeves cover the body and facilitate the bodily movements of men. But the poet's objection to paita/sari is that it is a symbol of chastity, sexuality:

When I see this end

of the sari

over my shoulder

I think of chastity,

teaches me shame

and whirls around me

a certain birdlike confusion.

Kongu

In contrast, in the culture from below, the attire is in tandem with the productive occupation of sudra and dalit women, for whom sari has never been ornamental attire. Besides being attire, kongu/sari is an inherent part of sudra and dalit women. Jupaka Subhadra, therefore, enumerates varied roles the kongu plays in the day-to-day life:

Like goddess Maisamma on the embankment,

the kongu round my belly holds my hunger

My sweat streaming as I work for wages,

my kongu wipes off the sweat on my face like a breeze.

When I tie vegetables, grains, provisions

into my kongu to carry on my head,

she twinkles like the moon gathering stars.

Working on the fields, tired,

my kongu doubles up as a sheet

for napping on the bare floor.

The contrast between the two sari-ends lies in the typology that the poets belong to. The elite feminists consider paita/sari as a symbol of slavery, chastity and burden while the dalit feminists consider it a part and parcel of occupation and life:

In the naughty rains, the cold as fierce as a tiger,

the hot winds, the simmering heat,

my kongu fondly wraps my face and ears

like the tangedu flower, forming an umbrella over me

she keeps my hair warm

like the shade giving tree

she comforts me

When I fetch water,

she becomes a rounded pad
below the pot on my head
she burns herself as a sooty rag at the stove.
While at work in the fields with my child
she holds my child like the niche holds the earthen lamp
my child playing all day in the dust,
she clears her streaming nose
she cleans the dust of her body,
as a cow would lick its newborn calf.
She drapes around me
covering like a thatch, the red of menses
As the snake stands stiff to the song of the piper
my kongu clutches my waist stiff
when I transplant, cut, weed, thresh
as in work, so in song
While sweating, while asleep
in work and at leisure
in sorrow and in happiness
in prosperity and in difficulty
like the dust on my feet
she is close to me
Where does she find time to drape herself around my bosom?
my soiled kongu is at work ceaselessly, as a slave

Subhadra also describes the patriarchy within dalits. Dalit men, who are themselves victims of caste, subject their women to suffering by inflicting physical violence:

When my husband

either in passion or anger

turns on me

he finds my kongu first, like a lump of soft butter

Kongu, she is a rag

the first casualty in the hands of men

within and without the house

who drag me for causing pain.

As a solution to the problem, Jayaprabha offers to burn the sari by means of rejecting the tradition:

If I have to stop

being the walking dead,

I have to burn

just burn this sari.

For Subhadra, kongu is a part of a dalit woman's chores, culture and comfort, because of which, she writes, she cannot afford to burn it:

She is no watch guard at my bosom

nor a burden on my heart

how can I abandon her in public, thus giving her a bad name?

how can I survive if I set her aflame?

Sari for the elite women stands as a burden. For the upper caste and middle class women, who are essentially alienated from work/production, the sari is a burden, an ornament, an adjunct. For the sudra and dalit women, the sari is essential since it is not ornamental.

The two feminist poems are antithetical to each other. The 'paita' poem privileges the elitism of women in its class. Jayaprabha employs the term 'paita,' which is suggestive of the region and caste. Its equivalent term used by the sudras and dalits in the Telangana region is 'kongu,' which Subhadra wrote about. Explicitly indicating the privileged caste and developed region, the 'paita' as a term privileges the elite women in three aspects: the upper caste nature, the developed region and the written word. In employing the educated language and the written mode of the 'standard' variety, the poem moves away in distance from the unlettered women. The 'kongu' poem, in contrast, employs the uneducated language in the oral mode of the Telangana dialect. Every word used is drawn from the language spoken in the mud houses. This aspect of the language, however, cannot be represented in translation. Concerning imagery, again, the former invokes the urban imagery while the latter draws richly from productive culture, agriculture, local myth making it organic and lively.

The elite feminists' attempt to objectify the issues of women lasted till the dalit feminists began writing themselves challenging the bases of the elite writing. In this respect, the 'support literature' by the upper caste men is better than the elite feminist writing. Several upper caste writers during the nationalist movement wrote about caste and untouchability. The support feminist writing by men like Gudipati Venkatachalam (wrote about women's liberty) and Tripuraneni Srinivas (brought out the first feminist anthology) is better than the elite feminist writing. Dalit women were, however, written about by dalit men, some of whom even assumed pseudonyms of women. Madduri Nageshbabu, for example, wrote with the pseudonym of Madduri Vijayasri. Dalit feminist writing came of age without being written about by the elite feminists. This aspect may be understood as the limitation of the elite feminists, who failed to write their dalit counterparts; and the success of the dalit women writers in emerging the genre, without being written about by their upper caste counterparts.

Notes

1. In the critical scholarship, the term 'mainstream feminism' is used to refer to the movements and scholarship dealing with the accepted notion of the generic category of feminism. Considering that the term inadequately represents what it should, I use 'elite feminism,' in opposition to 'dalit feminism.'

References

Jayaprabha. *"Paitani Tagaleyyali." Neelimeghalu*. Hyderabad: Swetcha Prachuranalu, 1993. First published in *Andhra Jyoti*, daily, May 31, 1988. Trns Velcheru Narayana Rao. Print.

Lalita, K, *et al*, ed. *We Were Making History: Life Stories of Women in the Telangana People's Struggle*. London: Zed Books, 1989. Print.

Shyamala, Gogu. *Nallapoddu: Dalita Streela Sahityam*, Hyderabad: Hyderabad Book Trust, 1921–2002, 2006. Print.

Sridhar, M and Uma, Alladi. "The Self and the Family in Telugu Women's Poetry." Ed Dasgupta, Sanjukta and Malasri Lal, *Indian Family in Transition: Literary and Cultural Texts*. New Delhi: Sage, 2997. Print.

Subhadra, Jupaka. *"Kongu Naabochemiida Kaavalunde Bonthapeggaadu."* (No Watchdog at my Bosom), *Andhra Jyoti*, 2007. Trans K. Purushotham. Print.

Subhadra, Jupaka and Shyamala, Gogu, ed. *Nalla Regati Saallu*. Hyderabad: Mysamma-Sabbanda Prachuranalu, 2006. Print.

Subhadra, Sheela and Rao, Bhargavi, ed. *Mudra: Vanitala Kavitalu*. Bangalore: Prism Books Pvt. Ltd, 2001. Print.

Swaroopa Rani, Challapalli. "Dalit Women's Writing in Telugu." *Economic and Political Weekly*. April 25, 1998. Print.

11

Does Shit Smell When Written? The Poetics of Faeces[1]

'When written, shit does not smell'

—*Roland Barthes*

Sage Vishvamithra ate dog-meat

to satiate his hunger.

There are those who eat

cows and goats,

horses and donkeys,

pigs and bandicoots,

camels and snakes.

But,

for the first time in this country,

a man had eaten

the faeces of another man!

Feeling ashamed?

There are in this country

those who drink human blood

man eaters too are there,

but there's no one else in the world

forcing men to eat human faeces. (*Shikhamani*, 27)

Some of the very means of the human civilisation became the sources of marginalisation. To be specific, excrement and animal carcass, if unattended, would have led to contamination and decay. It would have led to extinction of the human race. Therefore, it may hypothetically be said that cleaning faeces and removing animal carcass from human habitats made human civilisation possible. But these very two civilising occupations became the sources of dehumanisation and marginalisation of certain castes. In the social hierarchy, the dalit sub-castes, who have been made to attend to these tasks, became untouchable and un-'seeable.' Some other social groups like begging communities, rag-pickers, couch-sweepers, slum dwellers and scores of others living in mean streets and pavements are considered unsightly and untouchable; their sight recoiling. These sections defy categorisation, organisation and recognition: most of them are not enrolled in the voters' list for want of residential address; not organised under any trade unionism. The work they are involved in is not a formal or approved occupation and so they do not form part of a particular occupation.

These unorganised groups do not fall under the positive discrimination provided in the Constitution. They do not benefit from the welfare schemes that include subsidy, pension, housing, scholarships, free education and reservations. They are not paid attention to in the subaltern theories, marginalisation and exclusion/inclusion studies, which primarily address the issues of the 'visible marginalised groups' like women, minorities, aboriginals, the poor, the low castes, among others. Then how does one categorise them in academic parlance? The existing academic labels like subalterns or marginal do not characterise these groups. The character of their exclusion from all the organised institutions perhaps necessitates new terminology like 'sub-subaltern' or 'out-of-the-margins' to represent their socio-economic typology and character.

Marginalised or the subaltern sections are better off since they are recognised, and have the constitutional safeguard to their advantage. They are adequately representing themselves in the liberal arts and humanities creating new aesthetic space for themselves. They are not only written about; they are now writing themselves. Those who are outside the margins are not considered worthy of being written about by the mainstream writers. The question of writing themselves does not arise due to denial of education to them. The marginalised sections are now writing about those who are out-of-the-margins. This is an important development in the process of bringing into the margins those who are outside the margins. This paper seeks to examine this aspect by referring to the scatological narratives.

Faeces and Sub-humanity

People associated with scavenging are treated as less than human beings. In the European countries, where the prevalence of the social democracy accords dignity to even scavenging work, the scavengers are not looked down upon. In India, the lower the caste one belongs to the more one would be looked down upon. Of all the dalit sub-castes in the country, those associated with scavenging, known by different names in different states, and *safai karamcharis* (manual scavengers) in the official and trade union parlance, are treated in the most sub-human way; less than abominable animals like pigs. The aspects of economic exploitation, social discrimination and exclusion have been an everyday experience of the scavengers. Besides, on many an occasion, their occupation of scavenging becomes a source of endangerment of their lives. Bangaru Sridevi, an activist of *Safai Karamchari* Andolan narrates a gruesome incident:

> One experience stays with me forever. During the Vinayaka Chaturthi celebrations in Vizianagaram, a *safai karamchari* [scavenger] child fell into the water during the immersion ceremony. No one jumped in to save

> him because he was a *safai karamchari*. Touching him would pollute them. The child drowned. I can never forget this. To others, our lives have no value. It is better that [they consider] we die than they touch us. (Sridevi)

They are the worst victims of their occupation as they are considered unclean and impure. Placed at the lowest level of the caste hierarchy, the mainstream dalits also consider them untouchables. In this sense, the *safai karmacharis* are considered one of the most oppressed and disadvantaged in India.

Social discrimination against the scavengers is rampant. Living in the segregated colonies in the Indian cities and the villages, they are unable to make use of the provisions such as positive discrimination. One of the scavengers in Ahmedabad states: "When we are working, they ask us not to come near them. At tea canteens, they have separate tea tumblers and they make us clean them ourselves and make us put the dishes away ourselves. We cannot enter temples. We cannot use upper-caste water taps. We have to go one kilometer away to get water." (Smita, 10)

Faeces as the Cultural Taboo

The human excreta (faeces here after) are inevitable need of everyday life. But unlike other bodily needs, it became a source of social shame, and therefore it became a taboo in all the cultures. Its mention or description in art is a taboo too: "The strongest feeling of disgust is in general directed toward *human* excrement. Faeces constitutes a stronger taboo in art than other bodily acts and other bodily parts" (Menninghaus, 140). Mention of faeces publicly may be considered a taboo in Europe and other parts of the world; but not the scavengers. In India, the scavengers are considered a taboo more than the faeces; they are a matter of public shame and indignity. Therefore, the faeces and the scavengers are not written about in the Indian literature. Traditional Indian writers, who belong to the upper castes, believe in ritualistic purity. Since they consider the faeces and scavengers impure, the question of writing about them does not arise. By extension, this applies to the rest of the people associated with the 'impure' occupations. The absence of the 'impure' people and their occupations in the Indian writing is in keeping with the tradition of what the aestheticians termed 'silence' regarding the sexuality of women. Love and sexuality is written about by men more explicitly and rampantly than it is in the Western literature. But women themselves are not entitled to writing about their love and sexuality explicitly. It is a taboo to express it in real terms too. Therefore, they use silence as a trope to communicate what is not 'writable.' Like love and women's sexuality, faeces too is a highly silenced object. The words in the Indian languages used for expressing faeces as an object and activity, are circumvent expressions or euphemisms. The taboo surrounding faeces is manifest philologically too. The word 'excrement' comes from the Latin 'excrementum,' meaning 'to sift out, to discharge.' The word 'faeces' comes from 'skit' and 'skheid' meaning to shed, to split, to divide, to separate. Indian languages do not have words explicitly referring to faeces or defecation; words used for referring to faeces and to defecate are euphemistic or circumventive. Faeces and the scavengers are, thus, silenced and obliterated in the traditional writing. However, the social subaltern groups are now writing about themselves, and thus, faeces and the scavengers are now writing themselves.

Faeces in Literature

Mulk Raj Anand's *Untouchable* (1935), considered the first text to have dealt with the scavengers, is a groundbreaking novel for having a scavenger as its protagonist. The novel, however, is not radical in its approach to the problems of the scavengers. It is successful in gaining sympathy of the upper castes for the outcastes. Bakha, the protagonist is portrayed so fatalistic that he does not raise voice against the exploitative system. Bakha does not seek a solution to the untouchability in realistic terms. The flush latrine, one of the possible solutions suggested in the novel, would not liberate the scavengers. Tabish Khair observes that "the particular kind of individuality bestowed on Bakha is heavily loaded and socially limited" (Khair, 146). In spite of its limitations in etching out the scavenger as the protagonist, Mulk Raj Anand had foreseen the trend of the identity writing, a genre that is so powerful and authentic in the new writings. Other than *Untouchable,* no work of art in English, and by extension in the Indian languages, is devoted to the problem of faeces and scavengers. This is suggestive of the exclusivist nature of Indian literature.

In the light of the taboos imposed for cultural reasons, it is worth examining if faeces is writable. The question is, does faeces smell when written? Roland Barthes, though writing in a different context, would say no: "When written, faeces does not smell" (in LaCom). Faeces, being a part of one's being, is permissible in physical terms, and so is in writing too, in spite of the taboos. True to Barthes' conviction, there are quite a few references to faeces in the European art, literature and performance arts. The Europeans allowed it to be the subject of their writing, and it has subsequently come to be known as scatological humour. There are quite a few English works having references to faeces. Jonathan Swift's poem, "The Lady's Dressing Room" has a reference to faeces; in *Gulliver's Travels, Swift* contrasts Gulliver's repression of the faecal with the Yahoo's use of faeces as a weapon. Other texts dealing with faeces include, Jeff T. Kane's *The Five People You Meet When You Faeces Your Pants,* Jim Dawson's *Who Cut the Cheese? A Cultural History of the Fart* and Joe Lindsay's *Up Faeces Creek: A Collection of Horrifying True Wilderness Toilet Misadventures.* Physical description of faeces in European cinemas, TV shows, sculpture and other visual arts also are common.[2]

The Sociology of Faeces

What is considered a cultural taboo elsewhere in the world is not a taboo in India. For instance, the public display of sexual organs and genitalia in society or aesthetic forums, which is a taboo in any civilised society, is a predominant and visible aspect in Sanskrit and other Indian literatures. Similarly, the display of sexual organs and genitalia in the Indian temple architecture is so rampant that such display of obscenity at centres of spirituality is unthinkable anywhere else in the world. Whatever be the reasons the defenders of obscenity in the temple architecture may give, the nudity and the genitalia conspicuously visible on some of the Hindu temples causes embarrassment to the onlookers, especially to the children and women who accompany their parents and brothers. Those who defend the obscenity in the temple architecture are intolerable to the very sight of the scavengers in the day-to-day life. What is noteworthy is that there is far less shame attached to public nudity and faeces than those who earned their living cleaning out faeces. Indian writers extolled the public nudity using the most celebrated tropes. But the gruesome life that the scavengers and other social groups lead[3] could not attract the attention of the Indian creative writers.

Faeces and the scavengers have successfully been obliterated from the space of aesthetic forums. Faeces, therefore, needs to be understood in sociological and aesthetic terms to understand the question of boundaries and margins. The absence of scavengers from public visibility, like the absence of faeces, needs to be accounted for. The sewage workers, who include Madigas, Bhangis, Pakis and Valmikis in Andhra Pradesh and their counterparts in the rest of India, are outside the margins. Their scatological construct is obliterated. The politics involved in the obliteration is, writes Kristeva, "*not* [because of] lack of cleanliness or health that causes abjection but what disturbs identity, system, order, what does not respect borders, positions, rules. The in-between, the ambiguous, the composite" (Kristeva, 142). By weaning away the space due to the scavengers, canonical writers ensured that the language and the hierarchy in the society are not disturbed. The scatological narrative, an important aspect of dalit writing, serves the purpose of according due space in the aesthetic forums. As a part of this, the dalit autobiographical narratives effectively bring out the sociological aspects surrounding faeces. Sharankumar Limbale recounts an incident:

> After school we used to go to the river and sit on the

> sands to eat. Then we went swimming. The high-caste villagers filled their water pots and their women washed their clothes upstream. Downstream the kunbies and shepherds collected water in their vessels and carried them off. They also washed their clothes and bathed. Those who looked after the grazing cattle washed their buffaloes and bathed themselves. The water at the lowest end was meant for us.
>
> I used to stand in the river, collect water in my cupped palms and drink it. *One day some mother had washed her baby's clothes that sent a lump of faeces floating towards me.* But is there anything purer than water? The water flowing down from up river had already entered my stomach. I felt sick. (Limbale, 7)

This incident, took place in Limbale's village in Maharashtra when he was a school going boy, is suggestive of lack of equal opportunity to natural resources like water. Dalits were forced socially to use contaminated water leading to diseases and ailments. Limbale remembers another gruesome incident:

> Unless they gathered junk like broken glass, bits of paper and rags, and sold them, they had no money to buy their food. Kumar earned nothing. Oṇe day I accompanied Shantatya on her round to gather junk. I put my hand in the garbage, turned everything upside down, collected bits of paper. Or whatever I found and handed it over to Shantatya. *Sometimes I found a piece of crumpled paper and when I opened it, hoping for something, there was a lump of faeces inside.* Whenever I found a piece of candy wrapper, my mouth watered. A clean sheet of paper made me happy. If there was anything interesting to read, I kept reading it and Shantatya shouted, 'What are you reading? Come on, pass it to me.' (74-75)
>
> On the one hand there was the garbage, on the other, our hunger. The junk was sold by weight. I felt our hunger should be weighed instead of the junk, then we

> would know, at least how much it weighed. Perhaps we should weigh not only our hunger and stomachs but ourselves too. Did we weight at least as much as the rubbish we had gathered during the day? (74-75)

Vizhi Pa Idayaventhan, a Tamil writer, who had left his job in the municipality for he did not want to work as a scavenger, describes as to how it is an inevitable duty of the scavengers to clean the latrines in Nandanar Street:

> For namesake there was a bathroom in Nandanar Street. It had an attached latrine. They weren't separate. They had a mere dividing wall in between. The municipality had built it just to claim that the area had been provided with a facility. Nowadays it is not possible to bathe there. One can hardly even defecate there. It stinks too much.
>
> But even if the stink was gut-wrenching, even if it was worm infested, Putlaayi did not come for two days, the whole area would stink unbearably. Of course, the whole of Nandanar Street was not dependent on Putlaayi. After all, Veri Nayyakan Grove had become the official latrine. (Idayaventhan, 171)

Dalitisation of Aesthetic Forums

Faeces, which used to be abhorred, became worthy of clinical examination. It flies overseas for outsourced clinical examination. Assholes are operated upon by the doctors, who would otherwise recoil at the scavengers. The sources of abjection became the means of respectable occupation in sciences and medicine. But in aesthetic forums, the writers with traditional mindset are still resisting the idea of reading about faeces and identical themes. When science is forward looking, aesthetics cannot afford to be retrogressive. Just as dalitisation of science and medicine became acceptable and respectable, dalitisation of aesthetic forums in general and literature in particular too are increasingly growing to be acceptable. Scatological narrative, as an important form of dalit writing, too has attained respectability.

Dalitisation of aesthetic forums entails questioning the tenets of classical aesthetics, and expressing one's identity. Scatological narrative may be considered an effective means of dalitisation of aesthetic forums. For example, if silence is a trope in conventional writing, its obverse, the language could be an alternative; explicitness replacing implicitness, and so on. The physical description of what used to be the object of abhorrence is the alternative that the dalit writers construct. In one of the gruesome descriptions of the scavengers' lives, Vinodini, a promising Telugu academic and writer narrates faeces:

> So as to keep the house like a beautiful heaven, the silk-clad young girls, tender-eyed kids, cricket-playing youth, and the souls that pen romantic poetry would spend five-ten minutes in the morning at the smallest room that's their toilet at the backyard...It became slushy because of the rain. The excreta – that couldn't be accorded a place in the houses – would reach just behind the houses. The garbage of the house, stale rice and curries, papers containing the faeces of the kids, who were yet to learn to faeces in the toilets, menstruating clothes, fuss-ridden cotton used for wiping off the wounds, discarded condoms and secretly shaved hair – the entire horribly possible human garbage was present there suffocating in the heap one above the other...
>
> Seated on her feet over the heap of the garbage, she removed the shutter and kept it aside. When she removed the shutter, a dreadful stink wafted on the face of Jilakaramma like warm vapour. There was a big heap of excreta under the dry latrine. Since the inmates of the family defecated one after the other, the edges of the heap got spread over. The water used for cleaning their assholes got mixed up with excreta, and flowed like water-thin excreta. Jilakaramma, who was seated on her feet on the spread over of the excreta, was shoving the faeces into the full capacity of the tin-tray, and

> emptying it into the bucket. Since the tin-tray was worn-out, more than half of the excreta were flowing out before being emptied into the bucket. She was shoving it again and again, and emptying it into the bucket. So as to collect the excreta to the full capacity of the tray, she was shoving it with the broom, and so as not to let it flow down, she was supporting it with the broom so as to be emptied into the bucket. (Vinodini)

Compare this, for instance with the portrayal of courtly love, romance, description of nudity, landscape, war, heroism and revenge, which are considered fit to be the themes in the conventional writing. To write about faeces is, therefore, to break the silence; to break the boundaries; to enter the margins of the page, if not the centre.

By implication, the aspect of scatological narrative may be extended to the writing of the self by their counterparts involved in similar occupation. Because writing the self is but challenging the taboo. Writing the self by the excluded social groups is a sign of radicalising the writing by challenging the convention. The subversion of those social, cultural and physical 'rules' that govern the 'how,' the 'where,' and the 'when' has potential to create a space to talk about themselves in new terms. Whether the conventional aestheticians welcome it or not, the excluded social groups have begun to write their identity and self. There is no escape from the abject for the theoreticians if, to quote Cindy LaCom, "we may try really hard not to step in it [faeces], we are going to come away with some of it smeared on the soles of our ideological shoes" (LaCom, 11). It would be appropriate to conclude with an effective poem of Vemula Yellaiah who counters the social repression using the imagery of faeces:

> *With a bucket on the shoulders,*
>
> *a broom in a hand, and*
>
> *a tin-tray in another,*
>
> *my trace, where I set my feet on the earth,*

became slippery

outcast that is!

Drawing faeces from dry-latrines,

washing the stink and odour of time

in the manholes of sewers,

I would cap the stench

into a tiny casket.

Shoving off heaps of faeces,

offering a pitcher of water

for washing your asshole,

when I stretched out my hand for a coin,

didn't you call me filthy names?

Being scolded,

sporting an innocent face,

did I ever scorn any one?

Enduring the stench,

I covered myself

with the quilt of my occupation!

Being my own person,

I would plaster the face of caste

with faeces

till your caste-roots are crumpled, (Yellaiah, 64)

Notes

1. Presented at a U.G.C. sponsored National Seminar on Theorising

the Margins and the Other, organised by the Centre for Comparative Literature, University of Hyderabad—Feb 17-19, 2010.

2. Physical description of faeces in films, TV shows, performance arts include, "Along Came Polly," "Scrubs," "South Park," Mr Beans' famous comic strip, Bob Flannigan, Kiki Smith's sculpture "Tale," John Miller's sculpture "Dick/Jane," Gilbert and Georges's "Naked faeces Pictures" (selected as the best exhibition for *Artforum)* and in Bunuel's *Phantom of Liberty in which* the roles of eating and faecesting are inverted; people sit at toilets around a table, chatting pleasantly, and when they want to eat, sneak away to a small room. Read Cindy LaCom, "Filthy Bodies, Porous Boundaries: The Politics of Faeces in Disability Studies," http://www.dsq-sds.org/article/view/11/11

3. For a detailed documentary account of the plight of the scavengers, read Gita Ramaswamy, *India Stinking: Manual Scavengers in Andhra Pradesh and their Work,* New Delhi: Navayana Publishing, 2005.

References

Bangaru Sridevi, "Why should I Deny my Caste." http://www.newint.org/features/special/2006/12/06/dalit-women/. Web.

Idayaventhan, Vizhi Pa. "Nandanar Street." in K. Satyanarayana and Susie tharu, Ed. *No Alphabet in Sight: New Dalit Writing from South India, Dossier 1: Tamil and Malayalam*, New Delhi: Penguin Books, 2011. Print.

Khair, Tabish. *Babu Fictions: Alienation in Contemporary Indian English Novels,* New Delhi: OUP, 2001. Print.

Kristeva, Julia. *The powers of horror,* New York: Columbia UP, 1982. Print.

LaCom, Cindy, "Filthy Bodies, Porous Boundaries: The Politics of Faeces in Disability Studies," http://www.dsq-sds.org/article/view. Web.Limbale, Sharankumar. *The Outcaste,* Translated from Marathi by Santosh Bhoomkar. New Delhi: OUP India, 2003. Print.

Menninghaus, Winfried. *Disgust: The Theory and History of a Strong Sensation,* Trans. Howard Eiland and Joel Golb, New York: State U of New York Press, 2003. Print.

Narula, Smita. "Broken People," http://www.hrw.org/en/node/24485/section/. Web.

Ramaswamy, Gita. *India Stinking: Manual Scavengers in Andhra Pradesh and their Work,* New Delhi: Navayana Publishers, 2005. Print.

Shikhamani, "He is But a Faeces man." *Black Lilies: Telugu Dalit Poetry*. trans and Ed. K. Purushotham. New Delhi: Critical Quest, 2013. Print.

Vinodini, M.M. *Block, Arunathra*, a Telugu literary Journal (July, 2007). Print.

Yellaiah, Vemula. "Faeces." *Black Lilies: Telugu Dalit Poetry.* trans and Ed. K. Purushotham. New Delhi: Critical Quest, 2013. Print.

12

C.P. Brown and the Language Renaissance

The 'nextgen'—generation next—of the Indians, who are swayed by placements and career, are inundated in the mass culture of marketing, mobiles, internet and software. They may not even have heard that a person called Brown had served the cause of their mother tongue spending his entire life and all the money he had; they may not even imagine the quantum and nature of service that Brown and his ilk had rendered. May the tribe of those who know the kinds of Brown increase!

Charles Philip Brown (1798-1884), known as 'Brownu Dora' and 'Andhra Bhashodharakudu,' is remembered for the service he had rendered in Telugu grammar, prosody, compiling dictionaries, recovery of the lost works, printing of extant works and imparting free education by running boarding schools. An exemplary scholar, he had spent all his earnings, besides raising loans, on his mission of modernising and preserving Telugu language and literature for the posterity.

There were quite a few liberal British bureaucrats who served the Indian language. Among the important ones: William Jones learnt Sanskrit, and translated *Abhijnana Sakuntalam* into English. William Carey wrote Grammar of Marathi, Sanskrit, Punjabi and Telugu. A.D. Campbell first compiled a Telugu Dictionary, wrote Telugu grammar, and ascertained through research that the origin of Telugu was not Sanskrit. Others who also learnt the Indian languages during the British India were Benjamin, Schultz and Gordon Pritchett. Their purpose in learning the Indian languages was "to read books, and have daily communication with the Indians to have insight into the souls of the people." Brown belongs to this lineage of linguistic reformers and literary modernists.

The Europeans' interest in the Indian language had to do with the waning of patronage to the languages and literatures because of the crumbling feudal establishments. In the pre-British India, the country was strife torn with its caste and communal differences. Divided into many castes and tribes, Indians were too disunited to offer resistance to foreign rule. Following the Plessey war (1757) and the Buxar war (1764), the disunity paved the way for the foreign rule. As far as language and literature were concerned, the learned pundits were not willing to disseminate their knowledge to the people, especially to sudras and ati-sudras. Written Telugu language and literature were on the wane, which Brown described: "When I began the task, Telugu literature was dying out; the flame was flickering in the socket in 1825, I found Telugu literature dead. In 30 years I raised it to life" (Btown vii).

Language

Asked by Major General Thomas Monroe, Governor of Madras, Brown learnt Telugu to understand and serve the people better. Not stopping with the language proficiency, Brown mastered the language, grammar and literature. A polyglot in the real sense of the word, Brown was well versed in Greek, Latin, Persian, Sanskrit and Telugu. After his retirement, Brown worked as a Telugu professor at London University.

Brown, like Charles Wilkins (1750–1836), contributed to the reformation of the language. He changed and dropped some of the letters of Telugu alphabet making it easy to the common learners. Guided by the 'principle of economy,' approximation between spoken and the written form and learner-friendly approach, Brown simplified the Telugu orthography. The four letters that he had dropped from the Telugu alphabet include: *bandi* or hard *ra* replaced by the soft 'ra.' (It has however been re-introduced); the nasalised *arasunna*; hard cha and ja indicated by a mark above them replaced by the soft sounds of *cha* and *ja* as known today. As he was interested in printing the works, these changes facilitated the printing. The complicated Telugu script was due to the pundits, who were able to read and write it because of the tradition of learning. This could be because of the influence of Sanskrit as Brown would put it, "Sanskrit speech has influenced the Telugu language as much as, if not more than, Latin has influenced English." By making it complicated, the written Telugu was made inaccessible to the commoners. However, the changes that Brown had introduced, made written Telugu accessible to the commoners.

Literature

Telugu literature lost the patronage of the kings in the nineteenth century. The Tamil authorities did not respect the Telugu writers as Brown deplored, "The pundits expressed [to] me their grief, that the ruling powers regarded them as useless pensioners." Precisely at this juncture, Brown evinced interest in the Telugu literature, especially the works of Vemana (1700-50). Having written hundreds of verses, Vemana questioned the bases of religious orthodoxies, caste-based discrimination and untouchability. But hardly any of his verses were available when Brown entered the scene of Telugu literature. Based on what he had learnt about Vemana's oeuvre, Brown had embarked on re-locating the lost works of Vemana. Having hired some *raayasagaallu*, copyists/writers for preparing the manuscript of the lost verses, using his linguistic acumen and scientific approach, Brown had been able to recover several of Vemana's verses. Brown was successful in collecting and translating about 1861 verses of Vemana, and published under the title, *Vemana Satakam (verses of Vemana)*. This is no mean an achievement of a literary enthusiast, who belonged to a foreign country. Besides Vemana's, Brown collected the works of Tikkana, Potana, *Sumathi Satakam* and some other Telugu poems that were on the verge of extinction.

Besides recovering the lost works, Brown printed several works that include *Andhra Mahabharatamu; Mahabhagavatamu; Tale of Nala* by Raghava; *The Calamities of Harischandra* by Gaurana Mantri; Ramazrajabhushanudu's *Vasu Charitra*; Peddana's *Manu Charitra* and Srinatha's *Palanadu Veera Charitra*. Having authored chronicles and monographs in literary journals, he translated many poetical works. An editor of the *Madras Journal of Literature and Science*, he published articles in *The Asiatic Journal*. In order to facilitate the reading of several Telugu and Sanskrit works, Brown prepared commentaries for common readers to understand them.

Brown's contribution to Telugu language and literature occupies an important place in the literary history.

References

Veerabhadra Rao, Kothapalli. *C.P. Brown: Some Account of the Literary Life of C.P. Brown,* 1988.

C.P. Brown. "Introduction," *Dictionary: Telugu-English*, New Delhi: Asian Educational Services, 1986 rpt.

13

English and Dalits

English in its initial days was a poor man's language in England. It was not even a language, just a dialect. To speak and write English was looked down upon. Using Greek, Latin and French was a matter of status in England at that time. The status of English changed only when Henry IV made it an official language of England. Its flexibility and adaptability in terms of pronunciation, vocabulary and structure made it a global language subsequently. The entry and history of English in India too is distinctive. The 1835 Minutes of Thomas Babington McCauley legitimised the teaching of English in India. Macaulay believed that it was necessary to introduce English in India. He felt that the Indian people 'cannot at present be educated by means of their mother tongue.' According to him, Indian languages and literature were of little intrinsic value. Indian histories, astronomy, medicine and other disciplines were full of errors and falsehood. The continuance of Sanskrit and Arabic in Indian education system, Macaulay was convinced, could only harm both the Indians and British government. He recommended the closure of Sanskrit and Arabic schools and a withdrawal of all financial support to the teaching of these languages. No books were to be printed in Sanskrit and Arabic. He said: We must at present do our best to form a class who may be interpreters between us and the millions whom we govern, a class of persons, Indian in blood and colour, but English in taste, in opinions, in morals, and in intellect. To that class we may leave it to refine the vernacular dialects of the country, to enrich those dialects with terms of science borrowed from western nomenclature and to render them by degree fit vehicles for conveying knowledge to the great mass of the populations.

Das Gupta opines that establishing English language, culture, literature, and people as superior to anything Indian was the primary purpose of introducing English as the medium of instruction and as a subject of study. As early as 1823, Ram Mohan Roy had written to Lord Amherst that the Sanskrit system of education could only keep the Indians in darkness. Several commissions recommended that English be the medium of education. The East India Company implemented the recommendations of the commissions in letter and spirit. Many people may not be aware of the fact that the teaching of English first started in India way back 1857 when the three Universities were established at Madras, Bombay and Calcutta. (It took fairly a long time for the English literature to become a discipline in England. Cambridge and Oxford Universities allowed English as a subject after a great deal of resistance only in 1894 and 1911 respectively.) True to his vision and agenda, the English education created a special class within India – elite in education, culture and economy. In the post-Independence period too, McCauley's legacy of education continues thereby creating 'Western enclaves', inhabited by McCauley's children, within India and abroad. Side by side, there exist scores of children either entirely excluded from education or excluded from the English education. The exclusionist education is germane to the Indian tradition of education. In the feudal India, the unprivileged ones were excluded from education. In the modern India, the children are now excluded from the English education. Both the types, more or less, are synonymous. Pursuing this kind of exclusionist educational policy would be a loss to the subjects, and equally, if not more, a loss to the nation in terms of productivity.

Pedagogic Resistance

In the pre-Independence period, the teaching of literature passed for English language in the absence of language pedagogy. English as a medium of education, both at the school and the college level, continued without resistance. In the post-Independence period too English continues to be the medium of instruction catering to the needs of the elite classes, and upper middle classes too. This is so in spite of recommendations of University Education Commission 1948-1949, Secondary Education Commission 1952-53, National Education Commission 1964-66, New Education Policy 1986. But the academia grows intolerant if and when the extension of English medium education to all is debated. When, for instance Sam Pitroda, Chairman of National Knowledge Commission recommended, in his interim report, English medium to all from school to college levels; when the Minister for school education, Government of Andhra Pradesh proposed to introduce English from standard I, there has been a big hue and cry by the academia to resist such moves. Their opposition to English medium education at the school level is premised on the grounds: 1. That the primary education be imparted in the mother tongue; 2. That the children have to respect their mother tongue; 3. That the native languages need to be safeguarded from language endangerment; 4. That the cognitive abilities of the children can be developed through mother-tongue education and so on. These and several other reasons however are not applicable to the existing English education in the country! The English educated Indians have been proving all the above reasons wrong by excelling themselves, competing competently with their Western counterparts at the international level. When this is possible for the children of McCauley, why can't it be possible to the grand children of Manu?

English in Developing Countries

Let us consider English as a medium of instruction in Less Developed Countries (LDCs). There are two strands of thought. The first one is the rejectionist approach. In various post-colonial contexts, English had always been an elite language. It is a language of benefit to small middle classes and viewed as a prerequisite for access to the best educational opportunities and the most favoured professions, or top government positions. Imam reports that in Bangladesh after independence in 1972 there was a reaction against English that sought to restore the local language, Bangla, as the medium of instruction at all levels of education up to university. Bangla was viewed as central to the project of nation building for the newly independent state. In Sri Lanka likewise, Tamil communities in particular rejected English as elitist and secular. Tamils favoured education through Hindi, which carried identification with Hindu culture, whereas English carried the cultural baggage of secularism. In post-colonial Tanzania, President Nyerere proclaimed that Swahili should replace English as the medium of instruction in all levels of education, including universities, and at the same time called for a new emphasis on Tanzanian culture and identity. These are only a few random examples from various post-colonial contexts.

In contrast to these rejectionist approaches, other countries demonstrate precisely the opposite. A study across much of the Asia Pacific region found not only enthusiasm for the learning of English and its privileged position in the curriculum, but also for globalisation and the material benefits it promises. English is seen as an essential instrument in the economic development of many LDCs. In Malaysia, the switch away from English in the 1970s was ultimately blamed for holding back economic development and the policy was reversed. In Ghana, Mfum-Mensah reports a grass-roots rejection of any move away from English as the medium of instruction in schools, as parents see English as essential to improving the employment prospects of their children.

Indeed the widespread support for more, rather than less, English language instruction in developing countries would seem to indicate that the misgivings of those who feel uncomfortable about contributing to the process of globalisation are misplaced. Our students and their sponsors want English, and as already stated above, they want the globalisation that in many respects we question or even reject outright. Maley, however, points out that while the globalisation of English has raised its status as a tool of opportunity, it is by no means a sufficient condition for the success of the dispossessed. He writes that English tends to reinforce the power of the already powerful ... people whose success is bolstered and extended by membership of the exclusive "English-speaking club". Entry to that club depends not only on proficiency in the English language.

Inadequacy of Indian Languages

Indian languages are essentially inadequate for modern education. Primarily, they lack in the tradition of education. The vocabulary and the very intrinsic nature of the languages fall short of the linguistic needs of modern education. Besides the inadequacy, the Indian languages in written mode are alien to the learners. There is a gulf between what they speak and what they read in their texts. The written Telugu (as any other Indian languages) is alien to the learner. This is not to make an overstatement of the fact, but a cursory look at Telugu Reader of any class, as other texts, indicates that the vocabulary and syntax is quite unfamiliar. This is not true in the case of English: the written and the spoken English are mostly identical in vocabulary. To cut the long story short, the printed Indian texts are as alien to the learner as English is, and therefore, the concept of mother tongue medium does not serve the purpose expected of it. The inadequacy and the standard written mode of the Indian languages have a strong case for English medium education for all.

ESL, A Failure Model

English is not given up, but has been taught as a Second Language (ESL) in India. This is, however, a failure model. The ESL pedagogy may be partially successful in achieving English literacy – a doubtful ability to read and write English, but not for successful use it for conversation. In pursuing the learning of English, the Indian graduates spend about ten years, approximating to 3000 man-hours in the English classrooms. Yet, the English competency of the Indian students is underdeveloped, more so in the case of students belonging to backward castes, Dalits and tribes. In the ESL model, the teaching is grammar-centred, content-based and exam-oriented. The students, as a consequence develop an aversion for and phobia to English. English in the SL model, is more a cause of worry. Statistics of the results of any course, especially in the rural institutions, reveal that most of the students, who failed to get through the course, are bound to have failed in English. Attempts to introduce English as an SL from standard I is not going to make the scenario better. It may not be an exaggeration, but one may state it that learning English as an SL life long too would not raise the proficiency of the learner.

Tops Down Approach

The learners in the present education system are seen as a monolithic and undifferentiated community ignoring the aspect of their heterogeneity. The English curriculum, which is mostly English-centric, is alien, 'high' in content, cosmopolitan, national and also international in respect of themes and imagery. British literature is alien in respect of language, culture, ethnicity and demography. Therefore, a paradigm shift in the preparation of course content is desirable. The English pedagogy needs to be localised. Nativising English courses entails de-anglicising the cultural aspects of English, and incorporating native elements into the corpora of the teaching materials. The course content needs to reflect local situations, identities, ethnicity and diversity of the learners. Localising English curriculum in effect amounts to teaching English to the children through their own heritage and languages. English has to be taught through the texts of known and felt experience of culture, heritage, legends and myth, but not through the alien, strange, unknown culture. It is because of the latter approach, that not much progress has been made in respect of English proficiency. The tops-down approach, i.e. teaching through the native culture makes it possible even for the socially marginalised sections to learn English faster.

Empowerment English

There are two aspects of English teaching that alienates and consequently disempowers the marginalised learner. First, the content of the course, and second, attempts to teach

Received Pronunciation (RP). Teaching Standard English and alien content is a disguised forms of disempowerment. The marginalised learners, who fail to learn the 'Standard' English, rather get de-motivated. This is one of the reasons for the slow pace of learning. The notion of Standard English itself is dubious. English spoken in England is a small dialect constituting a mere four per cent of the world population. In India, there are more speakers of English than in the whole of Britain and the USA put together. Teaching of English through their own culture and heritage enables them to empathise with the subject. They should learn English by reading their own stories of deprivation and alienation. This kind of de-centered or localised English empowers the speakers of the language community who assert their English as the English.

The Africans have shown long ago the rest of the former colonies the modus operandi of decolourising the mind, culture, language, literature, pedagogy and the other social constructs. The decolonising African practitioners like Ngugi Wa Thiango, Chinua Achibe and several others have been drawing adequately from the indigenous and native sources to substitute the colonial constructs. Their attempts to debunk the notions of centrality or the standardised English have creolised English. The African writers and thinkers have shown the need and the ways of decentring the English language and decolonising the English curriculum. Influenced by the protest singers of the 1960s, black writers like Benjamin Zephaniah have reinvented a variety of dialects creatively expressing the black experience and politically resisting the dominant culture. As part of the experiments, the black European writers disturb the order of the mainstream. The same needs to be extended by the academics in decolonising the curricula in India.

English plays a significant role in the empowerment of the poor. In the post-colonial era, there is every need for the dispossessed living outside the margins to learn English for entering into the power centre. The kind of English to be learnt by the socially marginalised people is not the 'centred' language. They cannot and they need not learn the Standard variety of

English. On the contrary, what they should learn is the de-centred one; a Creole; a dialect; a variety and even a sub-variety. Because, it is the dialect or a variety that gives a voice, identity and legitimacy to speakers of non-standard Englishes. It is the non-standard varieties of Englishes that provide critiques of those who deny them their rights. Learning the standard variety of English amounts to the linguistic variety of Sanskritisation. Creolisation of English tantamount to de-Sankritisation.

English without English

Message determines the medium. It may sound an extreme proposition. English can well be acquired without English per se. As English in itself has no 'use' value, as it is only a means to communicate a particular content, it can be effectively be taught through that particular content. Institutionalised teaching of English entails certain negative aspects such as grammar, tests and exams and the notion of accuracy or correctness. Contrary to this model, it is possible to pick up English in the English medium system. The communicative approach comes into picture in this case. The learners are bound to learn English from the material as well as the teachers of the main subjects of their study other than English. A student learns English from her science or mathematics class quicker and easier than she would in her English classes. She would learn out of exigency. A need and an urge to understand a problem in science or maths makes the learner read in English and produce English utterances. Mathematics, science and social studies can be used as the course material for teaching all the four skills of English, namely, Listening, Speaking Reading and Writing (LSRW). The tests and examinations in these subjects can be used for assessing a learner's English competency. In the professional courses like B. Tech, for example, the teaching of English can be made more effective by making use of what the students read and produce as a part of their engineering papers. Therefore, the teaching of English through other subjects (mathematics, science, social studies etc) can be more effective than teaching English through English.

Conclusion

As regards education, India is passing through more critical phase than it had ever before. The field of education – the school and higher education - having been corporatised, the gulf between the caste Hindus and the socially marginalised sections has become unbridgeable. The social elites are, by birth and by virtue of their social status, entitled to English education. The socially marginalised sections are left with no other choice but pursue their education in the rural and vernacular medium institutions. This kind of discrimination is going to reflect in the social, cultural, political and economical unequal society, which does not auger well to the country. It ultimately leads to social unrest and chaos in the society. English education to the socially marginalised sections is the best means of empowerment and social justice. English education to the Dalit Bahujans can alone liberate them from suppression, oppression, violence and other forms of exploitation perpetrated by the casteist hegemony. The only way out of this is to make uniform English education mandatory to one and all in the country.

References

Lord Macaulay Macaulay's Minute On Education (1835).

Krishnaswamy, N. The Story of English in India. Delhi : Foundation Books, 2006. Print.

Gokak, English in India: Its Present and Futures, 1983

Radhakrishnan, S. The University Education Commission, 1948.

Gokak, V.K. *English in India: Its Present and Future*. India: Asia Publishing House, 1964. Print.

Study Group. The Study of English in India. Report of the Study Group Appointed by the Government of India. Delhi, India: Ministry of Education, Government of India, 1967.

14

Prosifying the Poesy: A Dalit Critique of Modernisation of Telugu

Sanskrit is the stagnant water of the Lord's private well
The spoken language is the rippling water of the running stream.

—*Kabir*

When a drop of honey touches the tongue,

your whole mouth is filled with sweetness.

The whole sense of a poem

should fill you all at once.

A poem composed with arcane words

is a dialogue

of the deaf and the dumb.

—*Molla*

The written word in the beginning imitated morpho-phonemic properties of the spoken word. For instance, there is evidence of written Telugu works, being close to the spoken language, before Nannaya: "It appears that literature also existed in Telugu about the same time, because we find literary style in the inscriptions some three centuries even before Nannaya's (A.D. 1022) *Mahabharatam*. During the time of Nannaya, the popular language had considerably diverged from the literary language" (Gazette). With the institutionalisation, the written word de-privileged and subordinated the original—the spoken word. The lettered brahmins privileged the written word and expected the spoken word to imitate it. The reversed modes of communication led to the binariness of the language forms and traditions—written and spoken; *marga* and *desi*; *grandhika* and *vyavaharika*. The alienated and corrupted written, marga, grandhika traditions needed reformation, which took place in different points of linguistic history of Telugu restoring dignity to the spoken, desi, vyavaharika traditions. This article critiques the processes and phases of the evolution of the modern written Telugu.

De-privileging the Spoken Language

Two forces were in operation in de-privileging the spoken word. One was Sanskritisation of Telugu and another versification of prose—prose, imitating the poetry.

The vyavaharika tradition in the written mode enjoyed its organic character till the emergence of the transliterators Nannaya, Tikkana, Errapregada and Srinatha, who were in favour of the grandhika tradition i.e., Sanskrit inflected classical Telugu. They considered Sanskrit the legitimate, and the non-sanskrit languages *mlecha bhasas*, the languages of the barbarians. The grandhika tradition commenced with the transliterations of the epics by suffixing the Telugu case endings, *du, mu, vu* to the Sanskrit morphemes. The subsequent writers in Telugu, belonging to the prabhandha period, continued the grandhika tradition. The transliterations and the early medieval writings used to be intelligible only to the Sanskrit pandits, but not to the educated commoners. The reasons for the promotion of the grandhika tradition could be termed more of extrinsic (social, cultural, political) and less of intrinsic (linguistic). The literary language had been stylised, distancing itself from the spoken language during 1100—1400. Tikkana's disciple Ketana

(13th century) prohibited the use of the spoken words in the poetic works making it more rigid. Inspite of Telugu being enriched by its contact with Prakrit right from the tenth century, the influence of Sanskrit alone had been validated, and celebrated as the sublime.

Another factor is strict avoidance of prose and using poetry for all kinds of writing like inscriptions, treatises and other documentary records. The pandits meticulously took care that the scholars and poets used poetry even where prose was suitable. Use of prose was discouraged for any kind of writing. Consequently, prose did not emerge as a form of classical literature. The writings of documentary nature like prosody, arithmetic, medicine and grammar were scrupulously written either in Telugu verse or in Sanskrit slokas. For example, Chinnayasuri (1806-62), a Telugu pandit in the Presidency College, who was patronised by the British rule, modeled his prose writings on the classical poetic language. *Niti Chandrika* (1853) and *Bala Vyakaranamu* (grammar for children) (1855), are the examples of the versified writing. His practice lent sanctity to upholding the classical language considering the spoken language as the degenerate form. Chinnayasuri may, thus, be considered responsible for the stilted growth of prose in Telugu.

Validated by Chinnayasuri, the classical poetic language won over vyavaharika, spoken language by 1919. He legitimated the use of the classical poetic language in the school textbooks and examinations. As a result, writes Blackburn: "Telugu pandits' control of printed prose ossified the language" (Blackburn, 12). The Telugu prose therefore ceased to grow for about ninety years (1850-1940) inspite of the best and concerted efforts of Kandukuri Viresalingam and Panuganti Lakshminarasimha Rao, who used a neutral variety—neither classical nor modern. Though the first Telugu work was printed by Benjamin Schultze as early as 1746 in Germany, Telugu prose did not change. Velcheru Narayana Rao, a noted Telugu critic and translator, argues: "Printing, which created opportunities for prose, for silent reading and for development of a modern subjectivity, was held hostage by the pandits" (Narayana Rao, 2004).

One of the primary reasons for the promotion of the classical tradition, opines Narayana Rao, was politically necessitated by the reciprocity between the brahmins and kshatriyas, who vied with each other for the political space. The grandhika poets received patronage from the kings: Nannaya and Tikkana, for example, were patronised by Rajaraja Narendra and Manumasidhi respectively; the latter in fact served as a minister. The brahmins in turn conferred kshatriyahood on the kings, some of who were of low caste origin needing the conferment of kshatriyahood for the political legitimacy. Narayana Rao argues, "the dialectic of mutual—brahmins conferring the status of kshatriyahood on kings and the kshatriyas making brahmins powerful by their patronage—is predominantly the story of brahmin ideology in pre-modern India" (Narayana Rao, 1995 : 25-26). The classical tradition flourished unquestioned because of the nexus between the political and the linguistic.

The social intention of the classical tradition had been to subordinate the speakers of the vyavaharika languages. Used as an effective tool of subordination, language became a demarcating line between the social elites and the marginalised sections. The sudras and ati-sudras, who spoke a language uninfluenced by Sanskrit, were treated inferior, uncivilised, barbaric, and so on. Not only that their languages were considered inferior, but were treated as unfit for literary writings. As a result, the degree of linguistic unintelligibility became a sign of scholarliness: the more difficult a text, the more respectable it used to be considered. The pandits, who produced the prabhandhas with competitive unintelligibility, ended up requiring *tika*, paraphrase for the understanding and enjoyment of a poem. A poem written in classical style was not readily understandable; it needed paraphrase or explanation. The classical tradition thus got alienated from the whole majority of the people, who constituted the sudras and ati-sudras.

Re-privileging the Spoken Language

The process of re-privileging—restoring dignity to the spoken tradition—had to do with political, social and literary reasons.

In the political domain, there was a transition in the feudal establishment. With the kings themselves asserting their authority in the name of divine king, the kings ceased to depend upon the brahmins for conferring kshatriyahood. The kings of different social hue acquired legitimacy ceasing to depend on brahmins for legitimating their authority. This transition was possible because the kings by then became stronger, no longer in need of the brahmins' social support. The divine king concept helped in reducing the importance of the brahmins.

On the social front, the mystics in the Telugu land, aiming at social and spiritual reformation, used language as a means of reaching out to the people. Realising that the high-flown grandhika tradition was a barrier to communication, the mystics chose simple and plain Telugu for carrying the message of reformation. The mystic writers practiced and advocated the vyavaharika tradition, though with limitations. The foremost of the mystics in this lineage was Basaveswara who originated *vacana sahitya*, readily intelligible prose texts, which propagated the caste and gender equality in the twelfth century. Another important mystic writer was Palkurki Somanatha of the thirteenth century, who questioned the Sanskrit works which are not accessible to ordinary people. The simplicity and sweetness of the vyavaharika tradition is put succinctly:

Telugu is simple, beautiful to hear

It reaches all, unlike these big words of verse and prose.

I will therefore sing in dvipada couplets.

Somanatha protested against Sanskrit. His protest laid the foundation of the low caste protest movements. Other writers in the lineage include Gone Budhareddy of thirteenth century, who composed *Ranganatha Ramayana*; Annamayya of fifteenth century who used desi metre for his Telugu songs about lord Venkateswara; Katta Varadaraju of seventeenth century who composed *dvipadas*, couplets; Potuluri Virabhrahmam, who along with his disciples, detoured sudra and ati-sudra wadas in the seventeenth century; and Yogi Vemana, who originated the sataka genre in the eighteenth century reaching out to the unlettered. The use of the vyavaharika tradition accounts for the popularity of the mystics; the grandhika tradition, with its complexity, accounts for the unpopularity of the Hindu philosophers like Shankaracharya, who remained unknown to the masses because of the unintelligible language they had used. The mystic writers contributed immensely to release Telugu from the clutches of the linguistic complexity. Inspite of the criticism of the vyavaharika tradition, say for example, comparing dvipada to an old whore, a backyard sewer, and a patron who does not pay (cited in Narayana Rao, 1995: 27), it flourished unfettered.

The literary factor that contributed to the simplification and popularity of the vyavaharika tradition is the origination of the inventive genres like satakam and vacana (prose), besides dvipada (couplets) that contributed to the re-legitimation.

The emergence of the non-brahmin writers and low caste artists, who acquired legitimacy during the reign of the nayaka dynasty, helped challenge the grandhika tradition. The non-brahmin writers and low caste artists elevated and adopted the folk art forms like *harikatha*, *veedhinatakam* (street plays), *kolatam*, *golla suddulu*, *bhajanalu*, *chenchu veshalu*, *yakshaganam* (musical play) *oggukatha, yellamma katha* and other ballets and plays. These folk art forms in turn revolutionised the language of literature. The Sanskrit epics, which were adapted into the folk art forms, could reach the unlettered masses. The reason for the popularity of the folk art forms has been that the complex texts (*slokas / verses*) are recited tunefully to the accompaniment of musical instruments like drum, harmonium, stringed instruments, and explain/ paraphrase them in the language of the masses. The audience would enjoy the verse recited tunefully and understand the meaning of the verse through paraphrase. Narayana Rao puts it interestingly: "The distance and the aura that Sanskrit had acquired were related to its unintelligibility. The Vedas and all the prescriptive texts of Sanskrit, including its venerated grammar, derived their power precisely from their being distanced from the ordinary person. However, their ideological impact would not be felt if they were not made somehow accessible" (Narayana Rao, 1995: 26). The processes of the modernisation of the Telugu prose, thus, traversed a long and chequered way. John Leonard sums up the process:

> The social reform proved to be the chief determinant of the direction of cultural change in the Telugu language and literature. The modification of Telugu script for printing, the initial effort at prose composition, and the introduction of new literary forms had occurred during the mid-nineteenth century, developed by the Telugu scholars who tried to control the language...The main motivation for this modernisation of Telugu was the hope that it would bridge the gulf which the educated elite felt between themselves and those who did not know [educated language]" (Leonard, 167).

And Narayana Rao sums up the process of modernisation of Telugu:

> After long and vehement persuasion by Gidugu Ramamurthy and Gurajada Appa Rao, and after heated discussions in public gatherings, academic journals and literary associations, the tide of public opinion turned towards modern Telugu. The pressure of daily needs in newspapers and popular journals gave rise to fluent modern Telugu prose. Great pandits such as Kandukuri and Challapalli Venakatasastry shifted their allegiance to modern Telugu. This was not exactly karanam Telugu but modern prose suitable for intellectual communication as well as artistic creativity (Narayana Rao, 2004: 163)

Telugu prose began to grow, inspite of the resistance of the pandits, since the nineteen forties. On the communication front, the mass media, with the emergence of the radio, TV, cinema and language newspapers, reinforced the importance of the spoken word.

Colonial Reform

The emergence of the Telugu prose in the late nineteenth century was made possible by the reform and the modernisation of the Indian languages by the English bureaucrat turned linguists. Necessitated by the British-Indian administration, the English officers had learnt the Indian languages to understand and serve the people better. Not stopping with proficiency, they mastered the languages, evolved the grammars and served the languages and literatures. Notable among them were C.P. Brown, Charles Wilkins, A.D. Campbell, who reformed Telugu; William Jones, Sanskrit; Benjamin, Malayalam; William Carey, Marathi, Sanskrit, Punjabi, Telugu; Schultz, Gordon, Pritchett, among others.

Guided by the 'principle of economy,' approximation of the spoken to the written form and the learner-friendly approach, the reformers dropped and changed some letters of alphabet, which used to be queer and farfetched from the spoken mode. They simplified the complex orthography making the languages printing-enabled and accessible to the commoners.

Brown, like Charles Wilkins (1750–1836), contributed to the reformation of the language. He changed and dropped some of the letters of Telugu alphabet making it easy to the common learners. Guided by the 'principle of economy,' approximation between spoken and the written form and learner-friendly approach, Brown simplified the Telugu orthography. The four letters that he had dropped from the Telugu alphabet include: *bandi* or hard *ra* replaced by the soft 'ra.' (It has however been re-introduced in schools); the nasalised *arasunna*; hard *cha* and *ja* indicated by a mark above them replaced by the soft sounds of *cha* and *ja* as known today. These changes facilitated the printing. The complicated Telugu script was because of the pandits, who were able to read and write it because of the formal learning and literacy. This could be because of the influence of Sanskrit as Brown would put it, "Sanskrit speech has influenced the Telugu language as much as, if not more than, Latin has influenced English" (Brown vi). By making it complicated, the written Telugu was made inaccessible to the unlettered. The changes that Brown had introduced made written Telugu relatively accessible to the commoners. The pandits however did not accord any importance to Brown's reform of Telugu, his commentary to the verses, which according to them were not 'scholarly.' This kind of resistance to the language reform needs to be viewed as retrogressive and anti-modern on the part of the pandits.

Followed by the Brown-reform, was the early twentieth century brahmins' reform of the language, started in 1907. This reform was commended as revolutionary. An English officer, J.A. Yates, who visited the north coastal districts of Andhra, was astonished to see the way Telugu was taught in the schools by the brahmin pandits. Having found it incomparable to the colloquial Telugu, he encouraged one Iyengar, a principal in Madras presidency, Kandukuri and Gidugu Rammurthy to reform the Telugu prose for teaching in the schools. Gidugu was already lecturing on the importance of the *jivabhasha*, living language. They cited Brown's *Telugu Reader* and Enugula Viraswamayya's *Kasiyatra Charitra* as examples of colloquial Telugu. However, conservatives like Jayanti Ramayya, Vavikolanu Subbarao, and Vedam Venkataraya Sastry were worried about the use of the colloquial Telugu in examinations. Kandukuri and Gidugu argued that there were no established standards for prose. They propagated *sista vyavaharika bhasha*, spoken language as the medium of teaching and for the examinations. Gidugu in particular prescribed the East Godavari variety as the model, which in the subsequent period has been made the 'standard' variety of Telugu. He has been considered the champion of language reform to the extent of celebrating his birth day, August 29 as the Telugu language Day.

Gidugu Rammurthy (1863-1940) argued in favour of adopting a prose style based on the language used in educated speech. Gurajada Appa Rao employed spoken Telugu for his prose fiction and plays. However, when it came to writing poetry, most of them used old Telugu diction. This was because, explains Narayana Rao, the "syllabic metres did not allow for laxity in the canonical shape of the word. It was not a just a matter of choice for the poet; it was the limitation of the metres. Poets, however modern they were in their ideas and images, still followed conventional metres. A tradition that had held sway for almost nine hundred years was not easy to abandon" (Narayana Rao, 330). This kind of preaching the spoken form and using classical Telugu is comparable to the English romantic poet, William Wordsworth, who proposed the use of "language near to the language of men," but when it came to his own poetry, he could not overcome the limitation of using the old diction.

Distinguished pandits like Chellapilla Venkata Sastry, Tallavajjula Sivasankara Sastry, Veerasalingam, Panchagnula Adinarayana Sastry, Vajjula Chinaseeta Rama Sastry supported the reformation towards the use of the colloquial language. On 28th February, 1919 "Varthamaana Andhrabhasha pravartaka samajam" was established with Veeresalingam as President and Gidugu as secretary. In 1924, Andhra Sahitya Parishat lifted the ban on colloquial language.

Madras government recognised Gidugu's services and awarded 'Kaizer-e-Hind' medal to him. Non-brahmin writers like Pattabhirami Reddy demonstrated his dissent through *Fidelu Ragaala Dozen* (1939). He carried vehemently his dispute with tradition to assert the breaking up of traditional meters and the grammar of Chinnaya Suri.

The net outcome of the brahmin-led language reform had been that the dialect of the prosperous Krishna-Godavari delta assumed the status of standard variety. The delta dialect, used in modern forms of literature and newspapers, attained the status of 'acceptability.' Thus, the brahmin-led Gidugu's school of language reform may be credited with effecting a shift from the Sanskrit inflected Telugu to 'standardisation' of Telugu, which in practice meant the educated spoken language of the delta region. Hence, Gidugu-Kandukuri language movement needs to be viewed as non-sudra and non-dalit reform, needing yet another linguistic revolution namely, dialectisation of Telugu.

Dialectisation

The genre of the short story played an important role in restoring dignity to the dialect. While Gidugu-Kandukuri language reform ended up elevating the delta language as the 'standard' variety, the Telangana and Rayalaseema dialects attained respectability through the genre of the short fiction. The Telangana writers like Ayodhya Ramakavi, Vattikota Alwaruswami, Kaloji Narayana Rao, Dasarathi Rangacharya, Suravaram Pratapa Reddy, B.S. Ramulu, Sannapureddi Venkatrami Reddy, Toleti Jaganmohan Rao, Allam Rajaiah, Kaluva Mallaia, Boya Jangaiah, Jukanti Jagannatham, among others; and the writers from the Rayalaseema: K. Shobha, Madhuranthakam Rajaram, Krishna Reddy, V.R. Rasani, Kesava Reddy and Namini Subramanyam Naidu and others wrote in their respective dialects as different from their counterparts from the delta region. Because of the rise in literacy and awareness, a shift has taken place in the genre. Ranga Rao writes: "with the spread of education and the democratic spirit, writers in impressive numbers have started coming from the other two regions" (Ranga Rao, 261). The Telugu short fiction underwent a transition when the writers of the two backward regions questioned the formation of the delta writing as *the canon*, and affirmed the use of the dialects, which are regional in character. The regionalisation of the genre thus legitimised the use of the dialects effecting a shift from the centre to the margins. However, the dialects—especially the Telangana dialect—which have been promoted as alternatives to the standardised delta variety, suffer from the limitation of being elitist and being upper caste in diction and accent. The accent and diction used by Kaloji Narayana Rao, recipient of Padma Vibhushan, considered the icon of the Telangana language and literature, is characteristic of the karanam variety as enunciated in a different context by Narayana Rao (2004, 163). Similarly, the literary and theatre movements and the struggle for the left ideological legitimacy failed to restore dignity to the spoken language of the sudras and dalits. Ramakrishna, in his interesting article on the topic too did not specify the failure of the left in de-brahminising Telugu (Ramakrishana).

The shift from the delta dialect to the other dialects, though considered revolutionary, is elitist in nature, needing yet another shift in the form of dalitisation of the dialects.

In Search of Prose

Malayalam dalit writer, S. Joseph, in his essay, "Poetry in Search of a Prose," writes about the inversion of the hierarchy of the genres—prose ceasing to imitate poetry, instead poetry imitating prose—in dalit writing (cited in Satyanarayana, 63). Inversion of the linguistic binaries such as standard-dialect; written-oral; etc., has been practiced in Telugu dalit writing.

Dalit writing after Ambedkar marked a significant shift from the dialect. Written in all the genres—poetry, fiction, biography and autobiography and the socio-political critiques—the dalit writings eschew traditional style of writing. The writers, mostly being activists, proved that literariness does not require using special, sublime, stylised language. They proved that writing can imitate speech re-defining the language of literature. This would mean the twin-shifts—shift from the written mode to the spoken mode; and from the oral mode of the educated elite speakers to that of the illiterate low caste speakers—became complete with the emergence of the contemporary Telugu dalit writing.

The dalit writing radicalised the language of literature thereby reclaiming the dalit language, which the dalit writers attempted at two levels. First, the use of the dialects. Though, it is not a new experiment to write prose entirely in the Telangana dialect, the upper caste writings in the respective dialects, were received with acclaim. But dalit works in the dialects did not evoke same kind of response because the dalit writers go beyond the dialect in employing the dalit register as well as the spoken mode as against the karanams' register and accent.

The dialects are enriched by the use of the dalit register, an authentic form of the dalit language that represents the dalit life. If the dialect is region-specific, register is culture-specific. The social aspect of the dalit life is best represented by the dalit register.

Another significant aspect of the 'proseness' of the dalit language is the use of the oral form, which best represents the illiteracy of the dalit characters and situations. Most of the Telugu letters that the dalit writers use are not 'acceptable' in the written mode. The oral form signifies the dropping of about fifteen letters that include ten aspirated allophones: k^h, g^h, ch^h, j^h, t^h, d^h, th^h, dh^h, p^h and b^h; four post-alveolar sounds *nj*, *nt*, *n*, *l* and dark *r*. These letters are characteristic of written mode, which are hardly used in speech even by the educated speakers. The writings of Vemula Yellaiah, Jupaka subhadra, Gogu Shyamala, Jajula Gowri, Yendluri Sudhakar, Kadire Krishna, among others, is characteristic of the spoken mode. The dalit writing from below dropped more than one fourth of the letters of the Telugu alphabet.

The properties of the ancient Telugu—sans Sanskrit influence—are preserved in the dalit culture because of two factors. First, the illiteracy of the dalits prevented the Sanskrit words from entering into their language. The textbooks, teaching and examinations provided for Sanskrit the inroads into Telugu and other Indian languages. The language of the educated therefore is more Sanskritic, and that of the unlettered sudras' and dalits' is free from Sanskrit elements.

Second, the social exclusion and demographic isolation prevented the dalits from the social contact with the mainstream. Consequently, the dalit language remained unaffected by the Sanskrit inflections. The homogenous nature of the dalit groups helped preserve the ancient forms of the Telugu language. For example, the *inter se* untouchability of the dakkalis is free from the alien inflections. The extent of Sanskrit words used in Telugu is similar to the demographic division of the population in the village: while the Telugu of the brahmins is most affected, the Telugu of the dakkalis is least affected. The caste hierarchy corresponds to the extent of the Sanskrit words and inflections. Thus the illiteracy and the social and demographic isolation of the dalits account for the 'proseness,' 'purity,' and 'ancientness' of the Telugu language. It took above a thousand years to 'prosify' the poesy, completing the full circle of language transformation, thanks to the dalit writing.

References

Blackburn, Stuart and Vasudha Dalmia, ed. "Introduction." *India's Literary history: Essays on the Nineteenth Century*. New Delhi: Permanent Black, 2004. Print.

Brown, C.P. "Introduction." *Dictionary: Telugu-English*, New Delhi: Asian Educational Services, 1986 rpt. Print.

Gazetteers. Revenue Department http://www.aponline.gov.in/quick%20links/hist-cult/languages.html pdf. Web.

Leonard, John and Karen Leonard. "Viresalingam and the Ideology of Change." Kenneth W. Jones, ed. *Religious Controversy in British India: Dialogues in South Asian Languages,* New York: State University of New York Press, 2002. Print.

Narayana Rao, Velcheru. "Coconut and Honey: Sanskrit and Telugu in Medieval Andhra." in *Social Scientist*. Vol. 23 Nos. 10-12, (October-December, 1995). Print.

Narayana Rao, Velcheru. "Pandits, *Karanams* and the East India Company in the making of the Modern Prose." Ed. Blackburn, Stuart and Vasudha Dalmia. *India'a Literary History: Essays on the Nineteenth Century*. New Delhi: Permanent Black, 2004. Print.

Rao, Ranga. "Afterword." *That Man on the Road: Contemporary Telugu Short Fiction*. New Delhi: Penguin Books, 2006. Print.

Ramakrishna, V. "Literary and Theatre movements in Colonial Andhra: Struggle for Left Ideological Legitimacy." *Social Scientist*. Vol. 21, Nos. 1-2, 1993. Print.

Satyanarayana, K and Susie Tharu, ed. *No Alphabet in Sight: New Dalit Writing from South India*. New Delhi: Penguin Books, 2011. Print.

15

Creolisation as Social Empowerment: Towards a Postcolonial Pedagogy

This paper attempts to examine the misconceptions of Standard English or monoglossia as opposed to the 'non-standard' Englishes or heteroglossia, and relates it to English pedagogy. The so-called Standard English is itself a dialect used by a miniscule percentage of speakers in England. By virtue of its contact with innumerable number of local languages over the world, English has been localised giving way to a number of dialects, creoles, varieties, and sub-varieties, sociolects and idiolects. When viewed from this perspective, the RP (Received Pronunciation) too is but a dialect. In the post-colonial context, in the context of 'writing back', to use a Rushdie-phrase, a new pedagogy of English needs to be developed. Disparaging the standard variety, the creoles and dialects need to constitute the curriculum of both language and literature programmes.

Centering and Disempowerment

The early 19th Century socio-cultural conditions prompted the founding of what has come to be known as the Standard English. English was used as a means of bond for bringing together the otherwise culturally disunited factions at that time (Krishnaswamy, 15). The attempts to achieve uniformity were culminated in the standardisation of English pronunciation.

Daniel Jones advocated that the pronunciation of the educated be standardised judging the other forms of pronunciations deviant and substandard. As part of this, Jones brought out his *English Pronouncing Dictionary* (1917) formulating the speech sounds and the corresponding symbols.

In the colonies too, the Empire standardised English education schematically. Its purpose was to instill the right 'English values' projecting the admirable British culture. Thomas Babington McCauley conceived it that the best ways of legitimising their political hegemony was through culture, for which English literature was considered an effective instrument. As part of this mission, select English texts were valorised so as to be incorporated into the English curriculum first introduced in the three Universities, at Madras, Bombay and Calcutta in 1857.

English became a discipline in England only in 1828 when first offered in the University College, London, and after three more years, it was offered in the King's College that was later on to become London University. Oxford and Cambridge universities did not allow English till 1894 and 1911 respectively. Because literature in those days meant only Greek and Latin, and English was considered less than a dialect.

In the colonies, RP has been projected as the model to be emulated in the Teaching of English as a Foreign Language, (TEFL), Second Language (TESL) or for the Speakers of Other Languages (TESOL). Eurocentric attitude – a sense of superiority of everything European – has been all pervasive. The language and literature curriculum in the Indian universities is essentially British in spite of the practical pedagogic problem that the course content is completely alien to the learners, who are, of late drawn from the vernacular-medium educated rural poor. The centering of English curriculum is complete and exhaustive even in the post-colonial context in India.

The implications of the centring of the English go beyond language and literature; it assumes wider ramifications in terms of power dynamics. The centering of English, or the attempts of standardisation, is a disguised form of disempowerment: the speakers of the deviant forms of the language have been excluded from the high culture and the power structures. It is worth noting in this context that the speakers of the deviant varieties of English are associated with such notions as illiteracy, rusticity, and perpetrators of crime, lethargy, parochialism, fundamentalism and other qualities that the West attributes to the people of the Third World countries. However, with the emergence of the post-colonial theory propounded by Frantz Fanon's *The Wretched of the Earth* and Edward Said's *Orientalism,* and the contemporary theories of Homi Bhaba, Gayatri Spivak, Aizaz Ahmed and the most effective praxis of the African activist writers, the empire started writing back with a bang asserting the native as the superior. The process of 'de-centring' English language and de-colonising the European thought has begun decisively.

Decentring and Empowerment

English, a language which has come to be spoken by 1,400 millions ceases to be owned by any of its constituent communities. All the users have a share in the future of English (Crystal, 143). Language is an immensely democratising institution. Once a language is learnt, one acquires rights over it in the sense the speaker can effect changes in it. English spoken in England and America constitutes a mere four and fifteen per cent respectively of the world population. In India, there are more speakers of English than in the whole of Britain and the USA put together. As a result of globalisation, English has assumed the form of as many varieties and dialects as the number of English speaking communities in the world, perhaps they are in thousands. Globalisation of English results in its localisation in terms of socio-linguistics. A globalised language, like the globalised culture, ceases to be homogeneous any longer; it comes into active contact with the native languages and culture where it is spoken. The new varieties of English assume the forms of dialects. With the centrifugal force in operation in the process of its globalisation, English acquires heterogeneous character at the levels of phonology, morphology, semantics and syntax. The speakers experiment with all the linguistic aspects of English developing dissimilarities with the Native Variety i.e., the Queen's English, which is always alien to the post-colonial speakers. On the other hand, the de-centred, or the localised English empowers the speakers of the language community who assert their English as the English.

Pedagogic Implications

The decentred English, however, is likely to pose implications for the pedagogy. English cannot be, and should not be taught in the same way as it is taught as a first language or a foreign language. The curriculum designing, content development, methods, materials and other components of language teaching need to be nativised. The nativisation of English language teaching entails the pedagogic aspects of the heritage, ethnicity, culture and the cognitive experience of the learners. The pedagogy of English, in other words needs to reflect local situations, identities, and diversity of the learners. When the learners of English happen to be the dispossessed and marginalised ones like the tribes and dalits in India, the problem is far more serious. Because, living in very remote hamlets, they are far fetched from the mainstream cultures and languages. Apart from the first language, the tribal children, for instance, are required to learn one of the Indian regional languages - Telugu for instance in Andhra Pradesh - to communicate themselves with the mainstream people living in the plains. English thus becomes a third language to the speakers of linguistic minority communities. This situation poses pedagogic problems in teaching it to the speakers of minority languages because it is taught pedagogically as a second language. This aspect poses problems of learning for subalterns like Dalits and tribals and those who belong to religious minorities like Muslims.

Therefore the subaltern and minority learners need a different strategy for imparting the language skills. One of the effective means of remedying the problem is to nativise English pedagogy. Put it simply, the tribal learners of English, for instance need to be taught by incorporating into the pedagogy their own languages and cultures. The approach should be to reach out to them rather than expecting the learner to adapt himself/herself to the mainstream pedagogy. A tops-down-approach is what is required of the pedagogy of the oppressed.

Pidginising the Pedagogy

Globalisation invariably entails localisation. The local aspects that might be suppressed hitherto globalisation get surfaced anew as a form of resistance to globalisation. The same is true of languages too. Till a particular point of time Standard English or RP remained a model for the learners. However, when English percolated down the middle and below middle classes, the centre loses its hold giving way to not only dialects but pidgins too. As cultures, languages too influence each other leading pidginisation. This is happening in English at a faster pace. The more English is globalised, the faster will be the process of pidginisation. When the working classes begin to speak English, English perhaps ceases to be English, and that is an inevitable aspect of language change. The other factor that is contributing to the decentring of English is the techno speak. The digital media – internet, e-mail and other modes of computer mediated communication – too contributes to this process. Dominic Dromgoole observes:

> It often seems that the English language is heading off in two separate directions. On the one hand, there are the wild abbreviated inventions of texting, all the different pidgin languages that are born on the street corner when an ethnic language bangs into English and the techno speak of modernity. All these separate strands of invention are blurring together to create a new English with hybrid vigour. On the other hand, there are the forces of reaction, pulling up the drawbridge to keep modernity out, all sitting around with tout, strained faces and trying very deliberately to excrete fashioned sentences like those of Henry James. (Dromgoole, 11)

The ethnic language and the techno speak across the world have hastened the very pace of the language change reducing English into pidgins. It is the pidgin variety that the modern generation seems to prefer to the Queen's English. A random observation of the English spoken by the contemporary Indian youth, for example, testifies to their preference for pidgin variety. This process of language change may be termed pidginisation, localisation or dentring English, which should form part of the post-colonial English pedagogy.

And what is more important is that the de-centring of English is happening more at the individual levels, and outside the academies and universities. Languages are changed by individuals not institutions. Ironically, the institutions and academies still suffer from the colonial hangover. The best example is the continuance of teaching British literature at the cost of native literatures in the Indian universities. In the post-colonial context too, the English pedagogy is still Eurocentric.

The African Ideal

The Africans have shown long ago the rest of the former colonies the *modus operandi* of de-colonising the mind, culture, language, literature, pedagogy and other social constructs. The de-colonising African practitioners like Ngugi Wa Thiango, Chinua Achibe and several others have been drawing adequately from the native sources to substitute the colonial constructs. Their attempts to debunk the notions of Standard English have creolised it. More than any other former colonies, the African writers and thinkers have shown the need and the ways of de-centring the English language and decolonising the English curriculum. Influenced by the protest singers of the 1960s, black writers like Benjamin Zephaniah have reinvented a variety of dialects creatively expressing the black experience and politically resisting the dominant culture. As part of the experiments, the black European writers disturb the order of the mainstream. The same needs to be extended by the academics in decolorising the curricula in India.

A look at the following two poems, one by John Agard and the other by Tom Leonard, is indicative of the extent to which they challenge the language center or Queen's English, the so-called pride of the RP:

LISTEN MR. OXFORD DON

Me not no Oxford don

Me a simple immigrant

from Clapham Common

I didn't graduate

I immigrant

But listen Mr. Oxford don

I'm a man on de run

is a dangerour one

I ent have no gun

I ent have no knife

But mugging de Qeen's English

is the story of my life

I don't need no axe

to split up yu syntax

I don't need no hammer

to mash up yu grammar

I warning you Mr. Oxford don

I'm a wanted man

And a wanted man

is a dangerous man

Dem accuse me of assault

on the Oxford dictionary
Imagine a concise peaceful man like me
Dem want me to serve time
for inciting rhyme to riot
But I tekking it quiet
Down here in Clapham Common
I'm not violent man Mr. Oxford don
I only armed wit muh human breath
but human breath
is a dangerous weapon
So mek dem send one big word after me
I ent serving no jail sentence
I slashing suffix in self-defense
I bashing future wit present tense
And if necessary
I making de Queen's English accessory to my offence

RIGHT INUFF

right inuff
ma language is disgraceful
ma maw tell mi
ma teacher tell mi
thi doactir tell mi
thi priest tell mi
ma boss tell mi
ma landlady in Carrington street tell mi

thi lassie ah tried tay get aff way in 1969 tell mi

sum wee smout thit thoat ah wuz revisionist tell mi

po-faced litarati grimly kerrying thi burden a thi past tellt mi

po-faced literati grimly kerryin thi burden a thi futuretellt mi

ma wife tellt mi jist-tay-get-inty-this-poem tellt mi

ma wainz came hame fray school an tellt mi

jist aboot ivry book oaped tellt mi

even thi introduction tay this Scottish National Dictionary tellt me

ach well

all livin lqanguage is sacred

fuck thi lohta thim

In both the poems there is a decisive attempt to challenge the notion of Standard English. By asserting the deviations in English usage, the poets questioned the bases of the Standard English. In the use of the creole and rhyme, the poets achieved a sharp expression of a new hybridised expression. What the poets challenged are some of the misconceptions of language: that the speakers of the dialects lack in intelligence and education; that speakers of dialects have criminal tendencies; that the dialects and creoles are racist; that the creoles are the 'illegitimate offspring of English', and finally that standard English is better than the 'un-standard' varieties.

By implication, what is questioned in these poems is the basis of monoglossia and the need for heteroglossia. In the context of globalisation of English, heteroglossia is inevitable. Language variation determined by region, race, gender, caste, class, education, profession and digital media is a *fait accompli.* It is not within the control of the Euro-Western academies to prevent, for instance, the emergence of an all pervasive simplified English form and style contributed by the digital media. This is so because users of the wwws, https and the .coms are scattered geographically and socially. The process of decentralisation or decolonisation of English has been set in motion irreversibly.

There is an immediate need for decolonisation of the English curricula in the Indian universities. Language plays a vital role in the political, socio-cultural and economic power dynamics, especially in the context of globalisation. In the post-colonial era, there is every need for the dispossessed living outside the margin to learn English for entering into the power center. The English to be learnt is not the 'centred' language; not the variety spoken by the oppressor. It is the de-centred one – a pidgin, a creole, a dialect, a variety and even a sub-variety. For it is the creole, a pidgin, a dialect or a variety that gives voice, identity and legitimacy to the dispossessed learners of English providing critiques of those who denied them their rights.

References

Crystal, David. *The Language Revolution*, Malden: Polity, 2005. Print.

Dromgoole, Dominic. "Punctuating the English Language," *The Hindu*, March 07, 2006. Print.

Krishnaswamy, N and Lalitha Krishnaswamy. *The Story of English in India,* Delhi: Foundation Books, 2006. Print.

16

'Our Exit from the Left was the Beginning of Dalit Writing' An Interview with Vemula Yellaiah

Vemula Yellaiah reflects upon his writing and autobiography as a mode of writing dalit narratives. He speaks on various aspects of dalit writing...

Question: Dalit literature in Marathi and other languages like Tamil and Hindi started much earlier when compared to Telugu Dalit writing, which became visible as a literary movement only since 1984, the year when the Karamchedu massacre took place. In spite of the fact that Andhra Pradesh is politically volatile with a history of peasant and tribal insurgencies, why this delay in Dalit activities and Dalit writing?

Vemula Yellaiah: It is a question of diversion from caste to land. We were diverted from fighting against the upper castes. At a time when we should have been waging struggles against untouchability, caste and for political power, we were lured by the Left by the hope of getting land, and they made us a party to their so-called struggle for land. Drawing their cadre from among innocent Dalits, the Left in Andhra grew to the extent of waging armed struggles in the thirties and forties, ultimately ending in the fiasco of the Left believing in the ballot for the first time in the world. They won the subsequent elections with a thumping majority. They surrendered their struggle for power. We did not realise that there was a conspiracy of using Dalits as cadre, as the upper castes were at the helm of affairs. Subsequently, they got lands and power. We remained where we were. It took time for Dalits to realise this conspiracy, and come out of the jaws of the Left. Our exit from the Left was the beginning of Dalit activities and writing.

Q: Does that mean the activities of the Left preempted Dalit discourse and movement?

VY: It is not a question of preempting; it is a clear case of diversion from the question of caste to the question of land, which we never had, and will never get in the present scenario. In the name of revolution, they created a kind of spell, turning revolution into divinity. For them, revolution is like god. Their writings too drew liberally from Hindu imagery and mythology. They will never account for the use of Hindu symbols in their revolutionary writings, though religion is opium according to their Marx. They are clearly not free from the Brahmin bent of mind. For a period, Dalits were under the spell of revolutionary writings during the period of the Abhyudaya Rachayithala Sangham (Progressive Writers Association) and Viplava Rachayithala Sangham (Revolutionary Writers Association). These two frontal literary organisations were responsible for the delay in Telugu Dalit writing.

Q: Do you mean to say that progressive and revolutionary writings that had its heyday for several years subsumed Dalit literature?

VY: Yes. They created a kind of magic spell among innocent Dalits. During this period, Dalits contributed immensely to Leftist cultural activities. The Left uses song, ballet and drama to propagate the message of armed struggle, and Dalits were at the core of this. The cultural troupes of Jananatya Mandali and Prajanatya Mandali were very popular in taking the message of revolution to the masses. Dalit balladeer, Gaddar of Jananatya Mandali is the best example of inspiring thousands of Dalits and Sudras to be a part of the underground activities of the Left. Dalit artists and singers who worked in the Left, could have otherwise created wonderful Dalit literature; they would have provided Dalits leadership, had they been not a party to the Left.

Q: The Left and revolutionary writers claim that their writings represent Dalits, and that Dalit liberation lies in a total revolution. Contrary to this view, in the recent past, several Dalit writers and activists have been critical of the Left, especially the underground ML parties. Criticism of the Left is one of the most important themes of Telugu Dalit poetry. How do you understand this paradox?

VY: The cultural troupes working in the Left without Dalits are zeroes. Dalits like Gaddar and Vangapandu alone can sing and dance the ballets. The Leftists used us for their purpose just as they used us as cadre. When it comes to writing, upper caste littérateurs never wrote about us; they can't write about us. How can they write about the Dalit experience? What is being written by Dalits now had never been written by the Leftists. Then, where is the question of their writing about us? How can an oppressor write about the oppressed? Their writings have never taken into account the major issues that confront Dalits.

Q: Kalyana Rao's Antaraani Vasantham (Untouchable Spring) is a case in point. This novel, written by a Dalit, is immensely successful in terms of sales. All the characters and the milieu of the novel are Dalit. It is published and promoted by VIRASAM (the literary organ of the Maoists). Is it not a case of the Left fighting for the liberation of Dalits?

VY: Absolutely not. Antaraani Vasantham is a revolutionary novel in Dalit disguise. It is yet another case of the continuation of the genre of revolutionary novel. It is like a green snake in green grass, to use Kancha Ilaiah's phrase. Except the fact that it is written by a Dalit, and having Dalit milieu selectively, there is nothing Dalit about it. In fact, I would suggest that readers should be wary of such novels which promote revolution in the guise of Dalit literature. As far as its success is concerned, it's like selling chilukaladanda, children's sweets at temple fairs. Antaraani Vasantham is a chilukaladanda in the fair of revolution. And its sellers are Brahmins. Brahmin Leftists, who prepared the requisite groundwork before its publication, are good at marketing everything, including revolution. This apart, the narrative of Antaraani Vasantham is based on the standard novel, which is not a trait of Dalit writing.

Q: This brings us to the fundamental question about the forms of Dalit literary genre. How is Dalit literature different from mainstream literature as far as form and technique is concerned?

VY: Form? Formlessness is the form of Dalit literature! So-called form or technique, shilpam as it is called in Telugu, is governed by Sanskrit and Western literary aesthetic. The primary task of Dalit writers is to dismantle these forms, and write from life. One's life in reality is not so ordered and patterned as is portrayed in mainstream literature. Dalit writers should instead draw from the rich resources of folk and Dalit forms of art like Sindukatha, Jambapuranam and so on. They should construct a Dalit aesthetic as an alternative to what they dismantle in terms of symbols, imagery and language.

Q: Defiance of the Sanskrit aesthetic seems to be an important aspect of Dalit writing. Can there be what is known as a Dalit aesthetic?

VY: Yes. The Dalit aesthetic needs to be constructed in place of what is rejected, the rejection of the triadic concept of *satyam, shivam, sundaram*. True Dalit aesthetic will be constructed through the replacement of the Hindu notion of Indian aesthetic by freedom, equality, fraternity and social justice, which are the soul of Dalit writing. As long as we don't create an alternative aesthetic, there's no point in criticising the Sanskrit aesthetic. Hence we need to create an alternative aesthetic. But it's not being done. The reason is that we are not allowing the dependent Dalit castes do so. They alone can construct the Dalit aesthetic when they start writing.

Q: We'll come back to language, which is an important aspect of aesthetics. But let us know what Dalit literature is. We ask this question because on the one hand there is a strong opinion that Dalit literature is that which is written by Dalits – the historical Dalitness, so to say. On the other hand, anthologies of Dalit writings include contributions from non-Dalits. Beginning from *Dalita Kathalu*, the first anthology of short stories, the two poetry anthologies *Chikkanoutunna Paata* (1995) and *Padunekkina Paata* (1996) to the latest ones like *Nallaregadi Saallu* (2006) and *Kai Tunakala Dandem* (2009) include the writings of upper castes too. The latter two, especially, are edited by Dalits. How does one account for this?

VY: Dalits rooted in the Dalit ethos alone can narrate the Dalit experience. Anything else is fiction. One must know that Dalit literature springs from experience, identity and memory. How can non-Dalits write about our experience, identity and memory? What they write is fiction, and fiction is alien to Dalit writing. There is no need for including the writings of non-Dalits in Dalit anthologies. Non-Dalits, especially upper caste people, are eager to be included in Dalit anthologies as they clamor for popularity, and want to sport a progressive mask. Dalit anthologists, who include the writings of non-Dalits, too are doing so in search of popularity. The anthologies edited by Dalits need not have included the writings of the non-dalits.

Q: In that case, of the fifty-nine Dalit sub-castes in Andhra Pradesh, writers from only two sub-castes – Mala and Madiga – are writing predominantly, about themselves and about some of the satellite or dependant castes like Dekkalis and others, who are yet to find their voice. You write about the satellite castes just as upper caste writers write about Dalits. How does we understand this? When the satellite castes start writing, won't they too consider you Dalit Brahmins?

V.Y: Yes. Definitely they will! The dominant Dalit castes like the Malas and the Madigas are equally responsible for the discrimination and oppression of the satellite castes. The Madigas, for instance, refuse to beat drums in the rituals of lower Dalits; they treat them as untouchables; they perpetrate atrocities on Sindu women who are made public whores in the name of *jogini*. The Malas too practice a similar kind of discrimination against their dependent castes. There will be a day when the dependent castes start writing and will accused the dominant Dalits of discrimination and oppression.

Q: If and when the satellite Dalit sub-castes are educated, and when they begin to write, do you think they will add new dimensions to Dalit writing since their experiences are different in that they live on the fringes, they are dependent on the major Dalit castes like the Malas and the Madigas, and that they are considered untouchable within the untouchables?

V.Y: Yes. What they write will become great works of art. They alone are capable of creating Dalit magnum opus. When they write, they will not rejoice in writing small poems to felicitate themselves. They alone can create masterpieces because they alone have the kind of experience to do so. Further, Dalit writers have only dismantled the fortresses of art and culture. But they have failed so far to create alternative symbols. They have burnt the Manusmriti and the Shastras, but did they construct anything to replace these? No! The dependent castes can and will construct new symbols to replace what is dismantled. They will do so by giving respectability to what is abominable in the present value system.

Q: Telugu Dalit literature picked up momentum in the eighties, and at a time when there was criticism that it was repeating itself, the writings of Madigas, fuelled by the Dandora movement (demanding classification of the dalit sub-castes for purpose of reservation benefits) made Telugu Dalit literature visible once again. Is Madiga writing too going to repeat itself similarly?

V.Y: Yes. We are already doing so to some extent. We are hardly adding anything new to what is already written. The reason for this is lack of self-respect and respect for one's caste. Most Dalits shy away from identifying themselves with their castes after attaining some sort of success in their careers.

Some writers imitate mainstream literature for acceptability and awards. They are in search of popularity. This is the tragedy. It has happened in other languages too.

Q: What will be the future of Dalit literature in that case?

V.Y: Dalit literature will never exhaust itself. Repeating oneself will not continue for long. As you said, when the Malas ran out of fuel, the Madigas began to write, enriching Telugu Dalit literature. By the time the latter get repeated, the dependent castes will begin to write more powerfully. And that's not going to be the end. Every time you run out of fuel, every time you repeat yourself, you need to learn from the more oppressed ones who begin to write; who have so much to write. The exhausted writers are not going to stop writing either. Instead they have to reinvigorate themselves by going back to their roots, and by learning a lesson from whom they had oppressed earlier. The future of Dalit literature lies in expressing one's asthitvam, identity, so as to dismantle and destroy the symbols of oppression forever. Dalit and Adivasi writing alone have the potential to do this.

Q: The Madigas have been fighting for classification of the fifty-nine Dalit sub-castes into ABCD for purpose of reservation benefits. The Malas who oppose this argue that it brings in disunity among Dalits. As a writer, what is your view?

V.Y: It is not true. Natural justice has it that everybody should have equal access to resources, and more so, in case of benefits sanctioned by the Constitution. As far as Dalit unity is concerned, our earlier silence was construed as unity. When we want our share, they term it disunity. Is this not the language spoken by the oppressive upper castes? One should keep in mind the satellite Dalit castes who are still far away from education and employment. It is the responsibility of both the Madigas and Malas to ensure them their legitimate share.

Q: In the recent past, Dalit women too have been writing very powerfully, mostly dealing with the experiences of women, suggesting the need for Dalit feminism. What do you say about this?

V.Y: Where there is oppression, there will be resistance. Oppression in a way, is counter-productive. Since Dalit women are oppressed, they will find their own forms of resistance. Dalit feminism is a form of resistance. Telugu Dalit writing has already produced powerful women writers like Jupaka Subhadra, Gogu Shyamala, Jajula Gowri and Vinodini who define what feminism should be like.

Q: Feminists would think that such an attempt would lead to divisiveness within women. Similarly, doesn't something like Dalit feminism lead to divisiveness within Dalits and thereby weaken the Dalit movement?

V.Y: No. As far as Dalit women are concerned, there is a great deal of difference between them and upper caste women. They are not the same. In fact, if Dalit women are the oppressed, their counterparts from the upper castes are the oppressors! Where is the question of unity between them? The question of unity arises when the so-called feminists first fight for the liberation of Dalit women. That will not happen anyway. Dalit women take part in production whereas the others don't. Therefore, when Dalit women create literature, it will be superior to Dalit writings by men as well as writings by upper caste women. Another reason for the powerful writing of Dalit women is their oppression at the hands of upper caste men, fellow women belonging to the upper castes and their own menfolk at home. Women writings by Dalits does not lead to divisiveness; it forges unity. Because the more oppressed always yearn for unity, not divisiveness. The foundation of Dalit literature or the Dalit movements is based on divisiveness from which a discourse of unity will be launched.

Q: To speak about your novel *Kakka*, there is criticism against this and your other writings as well, that it is highly unreadable; that the readers find it difficult to complete it. Why is it so difficult?

V.Y: I am happy that some of them admit that they don't understand Kakka. They don't understand it because they don't try to understand us; or they don't want to understand us.

Some of them pretend that they don't understand it. They don't treat us as humans. Therefore they will not treat our writing as worthy of literature at all. Those who understand us will certainly understand our literature. People who understand our literature and us are different people anyway.

Q: Some of them say that Kakka is difficult to read because of the Telangana dialect and Madiga language that you have used in it. Even the Telangand Dalit children, who study standard Telugu cannot read novels like yours. It is because education is not imparted in that specific dialect. In such case, do you think your writings serve any purpose?

V.Y: It's not their fault perhaps. To some extent it's because of the language of education that they consider their own language (dialect) inferior. Don't we refer to a dictionary if a particular English word is new or difficult? Students learn the meanings of new words from dictionaries. Therefore, dictionaries of dialects and social varieties need to be compiled so that those who are really interested in reading and understanding mudhouse Dalt literature can understand them by referring to the dictionaries. You have dictionaries for Sanskrit. What is the percentage of Sanskrit speakers? Dalits, for instance, constitute over 18 per cent of the population in AP, and Madigas alone constitute about 10 percentage of the total population. Our language is not taken into account in education. Does it not amount to neglect of Dalit language?

Q: Dictionaries are developed especially as a pedagogic need. But dalit literature...

V.Y: That's it. Dalit literature must be made a part of the curriculum right from the school level. When everybody is made to read Brahmin writings in schools and colleges, why shouldn't Dalit literature form part of the curriculum? Just as a difficult sloka or poem in Sanskrit or Telugu is taught, Dalit literature too can be taught and learnt, and understood with the help of teachers and dictionaries, if need be.

Q: Coming back to your works and the other mudhouse writings, is the difficulty because of the language that is used or because of the culture and context that are mostly unfamiliar to young Dalit boys, urban Dalits and non-Dalits?

V.Y: It is more because of culture. Language, anyway, differs from region to region, and can be understood with effort. The Dalit experience, culture and milieu are inevitably alien to non-Dalits and others, and these aspects form the core of Dalit literature. Readers need to understand the Dalit experience. If there is a will, one will certainly understand cultural complexities too.

Q: The very act of writing is to be intelligible to Dalits and non-Dalits too. Similarly the very objective of the Dalit narrative is to be authentic in representing culture and language. How does one resolve the conflict between readability and representation? Between intelligibility and representation of Dalitness, what does a writer prefer?

V.Y: A Dalit writer has to prefer representation to intelligibility. Cultural representation cannot be sacrificed for readability. The difficulties that readers might face can be overcome by effort. But if representation is sacrificed for intelligibility, it amounts to erasing one's own culture and identity. This is something that Brahmin writers have been doing. How can Dalit writers afford to erase their own culture? We will continue to write in this fashion so as to give our culture its due space, since culture is best transmitted by its own language. Can the culture of childhood, for instance, be represented in mature and well-formed sentences so as to be understood by adults? Message determines medium, isn't it?

Q: Do you think that all Dalit children should be taught in their native dialect? Since all Dalit children are not at one place, is it possible for the State to put this into practice?

V.Y: Yes. Dalits being the majority, and their language being closer to that of the Sudras, the language of education should be the native dialect of Dalits. The present language of education belongs to a miniscule community. The chairs of literature and learning are in the hands of a minority. This is undemocratic. Let the language of the majority be the language of education.

Q: In any village, the dialect of the illiterate lower castes is almost the same. How can we distinguish the Madiga diction from that of the other lower castes?

V.Y: It's not the same; it's different. The Madiga variety of language is different from the variety of language spoken by, say Dakkalis, a satellite caste of the Madigas. What is to be understood is that the more oppressed and segregated a caste, the purer is its language. This is because there is no scope for inter-language influence. The purity of Telugu lies in the variety of the most segregated castes.

Q: When asked, some elitist Dalits in high positions say that they don't have the Dalit experience. How do we define the Dalit experience? Is it different from the experience of other oppressed sections of society?

V.Y: The Dalit experience is bound to be different from that of other oppressed sections. It is defined in terms of the fact that they are not only ostracised, but are constantly reminded of their ostracism by several means like untouchability, living in the peripheries, and so on. To be a slave and to be constantly reminded of being a slave is different, isn't it? This is how Dalits differ from other oppressed. If the elitist Dalits deny this, it is hypocrisy on their part.

Q: Dalit youth of the second and third generations might not understand social and cultural oppressive conditions because their economic conditions are better, and their life is associated with an urbanised social milieu. Can such youth narrate Dalit experiences to contribute to the treasury of Dalit literature?

V.Y: Certainly. They too can express but in a different form, modified form. It is a question of self-respect again. How can they afford to forget the memory of the oppressive reality of their great grandfathers? An elite officer and a second generation educated Dalit, didn't Narendra Jadhav write the Dalit experience? His daughter too will write, but in a different form.

Q: Don't you think elite Dalit writers who are out of touch with Dalit experience and culture, are like non-Dalit writers writing about Dalits?

V.Y: No. Dalits with or without Dalit experience can write like Dalits. If the elite Dalits disown their Dalit ancestry, it's a different matter. A Dalit with conscience, though out of Dalit experience, is not same as a non-Dalit writer.

Q: Telugu has been given the status of classical language recently. What does it have to do with the language of Dalits and Dalit literature?

V.Y: The classical forms of language are still intact in the languages of the isolated Dalit castes. The satellite Dalit castes can point to the classicism of Telugu, not Sanskrit. A lot of research in the languages of the satellite Dalit castes needs to be done to explore the unaffected original forms of Telugu.

Q: How do you distinguish the difference between elite Dalit writers and mud-house Dalit writers?

V.Y: Elite Dalit writers in Telugu are outward looking, and therefore move from the self to the assimilatable mainstream culture while mudhouse writers are essentially inward looking, representing Dalitness. Therefore, writers belonging to the latter category alone represent the true Dalit identity that forms the core of Dalit literature.

Q: Autobiography has been effectively used by Dalit writers for representing the collective suffering of Dalits. Why is it that no Telugu dalit writer has written an autobiography except for Gurram Jashuva, who wrote Naa Katha?

V.Y: Gaddar is writing one. Women and the next generation Dalits will perhaps write effective autobiography.

Q: Can we expect an autobiography from you in the near future?

V.Y: Yes.

Q: If you want to write an autobiography in the future, will you use the same kind of language?

V.Y: I might modify the language because of the influences. Now, I write in my language, and I am proud of writing in the dialect of my mother. But when it comes to writing an autobiography, let me see what turn Dalit writing takes by that time.

Q: Boyi Bheemanna's play Paaleru was used as an effective tool to educate Dalits about discrimination during the nationalist period. After that, dalit drama like the autobiography, seems to be a non-starter. Why?

V.Y: It is a matter of appropriation. You might say I'm repeating myself (laughs). Our potential for plays and ballets was exhausted by Leftist theatre forms. Jananatya Mandali and Prajanatya Mandali minus the revolutionary element are nothing but Dalit theatre. Like our sweat, our art and literature too were appropriated at different stages.

Interviewed and translated by K. Purushotham and J. Bheemaiah

Select Bibliography

AUTOBIOGRAPHIES/NOVELS

Dhasal, Namdev. *Golpitha.* Trans. D.B. Karnik. Pune: Nilkanth Prakahan, 1975.

Faustina, Bama. *Sangati: events*. Trans. Laxmi Holmstrom. OUP, Apr 2009.

Gaikwad, Laxman. *Uchchlya*. 3rd edition. Pune: Shri Vidya Prakahan, 1990.

Gurucharan, Singh. *Masalchi: Punjabi Dalit Novel,* 1986.

Imayam. *Beasts of Burden*. New Delhi: Manas Publications, 2007.

Jadhav, Narendra. *Untouchables: My Family's Triumphant Journey Out of the Caste System in Modern India*. Simon and Schuster, 2005.

Joshua, G. *Gabbilam[Bat]* Trans. K. Madhava Rao. Hyderabad: Joshua Foundation,1996.

Kandasamy, Meena and Nisar. *Biography of Ayyankali: A Dalit Leader of Organic Protest*. Foreword by Kancha Ilaiah, Calicut: Other Books, 2008.

Kumar, Raj. *Dalit Personnal Narratives*. New Delhi: Orient BlackSwan, 2011.

Limbale, Sharankumar, *The Outcaste,* Translated from Marathi by Santosh Bhoomkar. New Delhi: OUP India, 2003.

Limbale, Sharankumar. *Hindu.* Calcutta: Samya, 2010.

Macwan, Joseph. *Angaliyat* (Stepchild), New Delhi: OUP India, 2004.

Mane, Laxman. *Upara: An Outsider.* Tran A.K. Kamat. New Delhi: Sahitya Academi, 1997.

Moon, Vasant. *Growing up Untouchable in India.* Trans. Gail Omvedt. *A Dalit Autobiography*. Rowman and Littlefield Publishers, Dec 2000.

Racine, Viramma. and Jean Luc Racine. *Viramma: Life of an untouchable*. Verso publication, Dec 1997.

Rao, Kalyan G. *Untouchable Spring*. New Delhi: Orient BlackSwan.

Singha, Shankar Prasad and Indrani Acharya. *Survival and other stories: Bangla Dalit Fiction in Translation.* New Delhi: Orient BlackSwan, 2012.

Sivakami, P. *The Grip of Change.* Chennai: Orient Longman, 2006.

Sivakami. *The Taming of Women*. Penguin.

Valmiki, Omprakash. *Joothan: A Dalit's Life.* Trans Arun Prabha Mukherjee. New Delhi: Samya, 1997.

Vyam, Durgabai and Subhash Vyam. *Bhimayana: Expressions of Untouchability.* New Delhi: Navayana Publishing, 2011.

DALIT SHORT STORIES

Acharya, Indranil. *Survival and Other Stories: Bangla Dalit Fiction in Translation*. 2012.

Basu, Thapan. *Translating Caste,* New Delhi: Katha, 2003.

Bhave, Sumitra. *Pan on Fire: Eight Dalit Women Tell their Stories*. New Delhi: Indian Social Institute, 1988.

Dangle, A. *Corps In The Well.* New Delhi: Orient Longman, 1992.

—. *Homeless in My Land.* New Delhi: Orient Longman, 1992.

—. A. *No Entry for the New Sun.* New Delhi: Orient Longman, 2006.

Gupta, Ramnika. *Hindi Dalit Short Stories*, Preface by Manager Pandey.

Shyamala, Gogu. *Father may be an Elephant but Mother a Basket*.... New Delhi: Navayana Publishing, 2012.

ANTHOLOGIES

Anand, Mulk Taj and Eleanor Zelliot. Eds. *An Anthology of Dalit Literature*. New Delhi: Gyan Prakashan, 1992.

Dangale, Arjuna. *Poisoned Bread: Translations from Modern Marathi Dalit Literature.* New Delhi: Orient Longman, 1992.

Dasan M., V. Pratibha and C. Chandrika, ed. *The Oxford India Anthology of Malayalam Dalit Writing.* New Delhi: OUP, 2011.

Mishra, D S. *An Anthology of Gujarati Dalit Literature*. New Delhi: Standard Publishers, 2011.

Narayan, Badri and A.R. Misra, ed. *Multiple Marginalities: An Anthology of Identified Dalit Writings.* New Delhi: Manohar, 2004.

Purushotham, K. et al. *The Oxford India Anthology of Telugu Dalit Writing.* New Delhi: OUP, 2015.

Purushotham, K. trans and ed. *Black Lilies: Telugu Dalit Poetry.* New Delhi: Critical Quest, 2013.

Ravikumar and R. Azhagarasan. *The Oxford India Anthology of Tamil Dalit Writing.* New Delhi: OUP, 2012.

Satyanarayana, K and Susie Tharu. *No Alphabet in Sight: New Dalit Writing from south India Dossier 1 Tamil and Malayalam*. New Delhi: Penguin Publishers, 2011.

—. *Steel Nibs are Sprouting: New Dalit Writing from South India Dossier 2 Telugu and Kannada*. New Delhi: Harper Collins, 2012.

Suneeta Rani, K. trans and ed. *Flowering from the Soil: Dalit Women's Writing from Telugu*. New Delhi: Prestige Books, 2012.

CRITICISM (BOOKS)

Ahamd Kan, Ali, *Identity Crisis in Dalit Literature. An Apprisal*. New Delhi: Pragun Publication, 2012.

Deliege, Robert. *The Untouchables of India*. Berg Publishers, 2001.

Abbasayalu —. *Sociology of Depressed Groups*. Osmania Univ., Hyderabad, 1979.

Abedi, Zakir. *Contemporary Dalit Literature : Quest for Dalit Liberation*. New Delhi: Arise Publishers and Distributors, 2010.

Agarwal, B. and Neeta. *Contextualizing Dalit Consciousness in Indian English Literature*. Biogreen Publisher, 2011.

Ahmad, Imtiyaz, and Shashi Bhushan. *Dalit Assertion: Society, Literature and History*. New Delhi: Orient BlackSwan, 2010.

Aloysius, G, *Periyar on Islam*. New Delhi: Critical Quest, 2004.

Aloysius, Imdayam S J., and Jayashree P. *Dalit Women Speak Out: Caste, Class and Gender Violence*. CUP, 2011.

Amar Nath Prasad, M. B. Gaijan. *Dalit Literature*. New Delhi: Sarup & Sons, 2012.

Ambedkar, B.R. 'The Great Conversion: Speech on the Eve of the Great Conversion Held on 15 October 1956." in *Thus Spoke Ambedkar: Selected Speeches*, Vol. 2: 140-65, ed. Bhagwan

Das. Jullundur: Bheem Patrika Publications, 1969.

Ambedkar, B.R. *Annihilation of Caste with a reply to Mahatma Gandhi*, in *Dr. Babasaheb Ambedkar: Writings and Speeches,* Vol. 1:23-96; compiled by Vasant Moon.Bombay: Education Department, Government of Maharastra, 1979.

Ambedkar, B.R. *The Untouchables: Who Were They and Why They Became Untouchables?* in *Dr. Babasaheb Ambedkar: Writings and Speeches,* Vol. 7:229-382, ed Vasant Moon. Bombay: Education Department, Government of Maharashtra,1948.

Anand, Meena. *Dalit Women Fear and Discrimination.* New Delhi: Isha Books, 2011.

Andhra Pradesh Civil Liberties Committee. *The Chundur Carnage*. Vijayawada, APCLC.

Arun, C. Joe. *Constructing Dalit Identity*. New Delhi: Rawat Publications, Jan 2007.

Arya, Sunitha. *Dalit and Backward Women*. New Delhi: Khel Sahitya Kendra, 2010.

Ashok Kumar Jha. *Dalitisation of Dalits.* Adhyayan Publishers, New Delhi, 2004.

Ashok Kumar, K.P. (ed), 1993, *Daita Gitalu*, Hyderabad: Sahiti Circle.

Aston, Nathan M. *Dalit Literature and African American Literature.* New Delhi: Prestige, 2010.

Azariah, M. *The Un-Christian side of the Indian Church: The Plight of the Untouchable.*

Bardan, Kalpana. *of Women Protests, Peasants and Rebels*. Univ. of California.

Berreman, Gerald D. *Caste and Other Inequalities: Essays on Inequality*. New Delhi: Manohar, 1979.

Beteille, Andre. *Backward Classes and the New Social Order*. New Delhi: OUP, 1981.

Bhagavan, Manu and Anne Feldhans. *Claiming Power from Below: Dalits and the Subaltern Question in India.* New Delhi: OUP, 2012.

Bheemaiah, J. ed. *Dalits and Social Marginalisation.* Jaipur: Avishkar Publishers, 2012.

Bhai, P. Nirmal. *Harijan Women in Independent India*. New Delhi: B.R. Publishing Corporation, 1986.

Bhanu, G. *Telugu Navala Sahityam-Harijana-bhyudayam*, (Telugu), Unpublished Ph.D. Thesis, Nagarjuna Univ., 1987.

Bharathi, Thummapudi. *A History of Telugu Dalit Literature.* Kalpaz Publications, 2008.

Bhole, R.R. *An Untouchable Speaks*. London: Britain Publishing Company, 1944.

Biswas, Swapan Kumar. *Gods, False Gods and The Untouchables*. New Delhi: Orion, 1998.

Buck, David C and Kannan. *Tamil Dalit Literature: My own Experience*, Pondicherry: French Institute of Pondicherry, 2011.

Chandrabhan, Prasad. *Dalit Dairy 1999-2003: Reflections on Apartheid in India.* New Delhi: Navayana Publications, 2009.

Chinna Rao, Yagati, 1992, *Literature and Ideology: A Study of Telugu Literature*, 1920-42, Unpublished M.Phil. Dissertation, Jawaharlal Nehru Univ.

Chinna Rao, Yagati, 1999b, 'The World of Untouchables in Medieval Telugu Literature: A Study of Vemana." in R. Soma Reddy, M Radhakrishna Sharma and A Satyanarayana (eds.), *Social Evils in Andhra Desa: 17th and 18th Centuries AD*, (Proceedings of the Seminar), Hyderabad, Department of History, Osmania Univ.

Clarke, Sathianathan et al. *Dalit Theology in the Twenty-First Century: Discordant Voices, Discerning Pathways*. New Delhi: OUP, 2010.

Clarke, Sathianathan. *Dalits and Christianity*. New Delhi: OUP, 1998. *Converts*. Bangalore, 1985.

Dangle, Arjun, ed. *No Entry for the New Sun: Translations from Modern Marathi Dalit Poetry,* New Delhi: Disha Books, 1992.

Debjani, Ganguly. *Caste and Dalit Lifeworlds: Postcolonial Perspectives*, New Delhi: Orient Longman, 2008.

Debjani, Ganguly. Caste, Colonialism and Counter-Modernity: Notes on a Postcolonial Hermeneutics of Caste, London: Routledge.

Forrester, Duncan B., 1991, 'The Depressed Classes and Conversion to Christianity: 1860-1960' in G.A. Oddie (Ed.), *Religion in South Asia: Religious Conversion and Revival Movements in South Asia in Medieval and Modern Times*, New Delhi, Manohar, (First Published in 1977).

Ghosh, G K. *Dalit Women*. New Delhi: APH Publishing House, 1997.

Goopt, Nandini. *Swami Acchutanand and The Adi-Hindu Movement.* New Delhi: Critical Quest, 2006.

Subordination and the Dalit Challenge, Vol. 2. New Delhi: Sage Publications, 2001, 160-194.

Hardmann, Eva Maria. *The Dalit Movement in India: Local Practices Gobal Connections*. New Delhi: OUP, 2011.

Hazari (1968). *Untouchable: The Autobiography of an Indian Outcaste*. New York: Frederick A. Praeger Publishers.

Ilaiah, Kancha. *Why I Am Not a Hindu: A Sudra Critique of Hindutva Philosophy, Culture and Political Economy.* Calcutta: Samya, 1996.

Ilaiah, Kancha, *God as Political Philosopher: Buddha's Challenge to Brahmanism*, Kolkata: Samya, 2004.

Jeffrelot, Christopher. *Dr. Ambedkar and Untouchability*. New Delhi: Orient BlackSwan, 2005.

Jogdand, P. G. *Dalit Women: Issues and Perspectives.* New Delhi: Gyan Publishing House, 1995.

Julia Kristeva, *The Powers of Horror,* New York: Columbia UP, 1982, 142.

Khare, R. S. *The Untouchable as Himself: Ideology, Identity and Pragmatism among the Lucknow Chamars.* Cambridge, 1984.

Klass, Morton, 1993, Caste in Caste: the Emergence of the South Asian Social System, New Delhi, Manohar, 2010.

Kumar, Satendra. *Socio Political Concerns in Dalit Literature: A Critical Survey.* New Delhi: Yking Books, 2011.

Kumar, Satendra. *Unheard Voices of Dalit Literature*. New Delhi: Yking Books, 2011.

Limbale, Sharankumar. *Towards an Aesthetic of Dalit Literature.* Hyderabad: Orient Longman, 2008.

Limbale, Sharankumar. *Towards an Aesthetic of Dalit Literature: History,Controversies and Considerations.* Hyderabad; Orient Longman, 2004.

Limbale, Sharankumar. *Towards an Aesthetic of Dalit Literature: History, Controversies and Considerations*, Orient Longman, 2004.

Limbale, Sharankumar. *Towards an Aesthetic of Dalit Literature: History, Controversies and Considerations,* trans Alock Mukherjee. Hyderabad: Orient Longman, 2004.

Magdum, Ajit B. *Comparative Literature: Dalit Poetry and African American Poetry*. Roli Books, 2009.

Mahar, Micheal. *The Untouchables in Contemporary India*. New Delhi: Rawat Publications, 1998.

Mahida, Beena A. *Indian Dalit Literature*. New Delhi: Sarth Publication, 2011.

Malhotra, Rajiv and Aravindan Neelakandan. *Breaking India: Western Interventions in Dravidian and Dalit Faculties*. Amaryllis, 2010.

Mane, Vasudha. "Recent Marathi Writings." *Indian Litreature,* 17(4), 1974: 98-103.

Mangoo Ram, Ronki Ram. *Ad Dharm and The Dalit Movement in Punjab*. New Delhi: Critical Quest, 2008.

Mani, Braj Ranjan. *Debrahmanishing History: Dominance and Resistance in Indian Society*. New Delhi: Manohar, 2005.

Massania, Ramsharan. *Major Trends and Development in Dalit Politics*. New Delhi: Cyber Tech Publication, 2008.

Massay, James. *Towards Dalit Hermeneutics: Rereading the text, the History and the Literature*. Ispck, 1994.

Micheal, S M. *Dalit in Modern India: Visions and Values*. Sage India, May 2007.

Misra, Aswini Kumar. "Voices of Dalits in South Asian Literature." http//www.sasnet.lu.se. Web.

Mittal, Mukta. *Dalit Women in India: Survival and Current Dilemma*. New Delhi: Arise Publishers and Distributors, 2010.

Moffatt, Micheal. *An Untouchable Community in South India: Structure and Consensus,* Princeton, Princeton Univ. Press, 1979.

Mohanty, Manoranjan. *Caste, Class and Gender*. New Delhi: Sage Publications, 2004.

More, Dado. "Dalit Writing Achievement and Prospects." in Bojja Tharakam, Ed. *The First All India Dalit Writers Conference*, Hyderabad, Dr B.R. Ambedkar Memorial Trust, 1994.

Mosse, D. (1996). *Dalit Literature in Western India: An Annotated Bibliography*. Surat: Centre for Social Studies.

Mukherjee, Prabhati, *Beyond the Four Varnas: The Untouchables in India.* Shimla: Indian Institute of Advanced Study,1988.

Mulk Raj and Eleanor Zelliot, eds. *An Anthology of Dalit Literature.* New Delhi: Gyan, 1992.

Murali Manohar, D. *Critical Essays on Dalit Literature.* New Delhi: Atlantic, 2013.

Naik, D. Ramalu, 1992. *M.V. Bhagya Reddi Varma's Life and Mission: A Study,* Unpublished M Phil. Disseratation, Osmania Univ.

Nalini Iyer and Bonnie Zare ed. *Other Tongues: Rethinking the Language Debates in India.* NY: Rodopi B.V, 2009.

Natarajan, Srividya and Aparajitha Nina. *A Gardener in the Wasteland: Jotiba Phule's Fight for Liberty.* New Delhi: Navayana Publications, 2011.

Ojha, R. *Dalit Women in India*. New Delhi: Akansha Publishing House, 2011.

Omvedt, Gail. *Ambedkar: Towards an Enlightened India*. New Delhi: Penguin, 2008.

Omvedt, Gail. *Buddhism in India*. New Delhi: Sage India, 2003.

Omvedt, Gail. *Dalit and the Democratic Revolution: Dr Ambedkar and The Dalit Movement in Colonial India.* New Delhi: Sage India, 1994.

Omvedt, Gail. *Dalit Visions (revised edition).* New Delhi: Orient BlackSwan, 2010.

Omvedt, Gail. *Dalit Visions : Tracts for the Times.* Delhi: Orient Longman, 1995.

Omvedt, Gail. *Dalit Visions: The Anti-Caste Movement and the Construction of an Indian Identity,* New Delhi : Orient Longman, 2006.

Omvedt, Gail. *Dalits and the Democratic Revolution: Dr. Ambedkar and the Dalit Movement in Colonial India.* Delhi: Sage, 1994.

Omvedt, Gail. *Dalits and the Democratic Revolution: Dr. Ambedkar and the Dalit Movement in Colonial India.* Delhi: Sage, 1994, 16.

Omvedt, Gail. "Indian Feminism and the Patriarchy of Caste." *Himal* (February, 2003).

Poddar, Bhagirath. *The Untouchables in Modern India.* New Delhi: Sarup Book Publishers, 2001.

Pradeep, K. Sharma. *Dalit Politics and Literature Hardcover.* New Delhi: Shipra Publications, 2006.

Prasad, Amarnath. *Dalit Literature: A Critical Exploration.* New Delhi: Sarup Books, 2007. Press, Berkeley, 1990.

Randhawa, Harbir Singh. *Dalit Literature.* New Delhi: Sarup Book Publishers, 2010.

Rege, Sharmila. *Women Writing Caste: Testimonios of Dalit Women in Maharashtra.* New Delhi: Zubaan Books, 2004.

Rege, Sharmila. *Writing Caste / Writing Gender: Narrating Dalit Womens Testimonios.* New Delhi: Zubaan Books, 2004.

Robinson, Rowena and Joseph Marianus. *Margins of Faith: Dalit and Tribal Christianity in India.* New Delhi: Sage India, Aug 2010.

Roy, Ramashray. *Gandhi and Ambedkar: A Study in Contrast.* New Delhi: Shipra Publications, 2006.

Sachchidananda. *Dalit Women on the Move: The Bihar Scenario.* New Delhi: Serials Publications, 2005.

Sadangi, Himansucharan. *Dalit the Downtrodden of India.* New Delhi: Gyan Books, 2004.

Sharma, Pradeep K. *Dalit Politics and Literature.* New Delhi: Shipra Publications, 2006.

Sharma, Trilok. *Dalit Women: Issues and Perspectives.* New Delhi: Sonali Publications, 2011.

Singh, A K. *Crime Against Dalit Women.* New Delhi: DSP Publishing House, 2011.

Singh, Karan, and Amod Kumar Rai. *Dalit Literature: Challenges and Potentialities.* New Delhi: Creative Books, 2010.

Singh, S K. *Dalit Women: Socio Economic Status and Issues.* New Royal Books, 2000. Social Institute, New Delhi, 1997.

Tiwari, B N. *The Making of Dalit Public in North India – U P, 1950-Present.* New Delhi: OUP, 2011.

Vishwanathan, S. *Dalits in Dravidian Land: Frontline Reports on Anti Dalit.* New Delhi: Navayana Publications, 2009.

Vishwanathan, Seetha. *Patterns of Oppression in African and Telugu Dalit Poetry: A Comparative Study.* Diss. Univ. of Hyderabad, (Supervisor: Alladi Uma), 2006.

Vinayakala, H. *The Discourse of Dalit Feminism: A Study of Bama's Sivakami and Gogu Shyamala.*Diss. EFLU, Hyderabad, 2012.

Yadav, Karan. Dalit Literature: Challenges and Potentialities (Creative New Literature Series-113), New Delhi: Creative Books, 2009.

CRITICISM (ARTICLES)

Chandra Mouli, T.S. "Dalit Poetry in Telugu." *Special Issue on Dalit Literature.* Tiruvanantapuram:The Word Plus, December, 2005.

Dangle, Arjun. "Dalit Literature, Past, Present and Future." trans Avinash S.Pandit and Daya Agarwal, in *Poisoned Bread: Translations from Modern Marathi Dalit Literature,* ed Arjun Dangle: Orient Longman, 1992.

Debjani, Ganguly. "Can the Dalit Speak: Of Caste, Postcoloniality and the New Humanities." *South Asia: Journal of South Asian Studies*. Vol. XXIII, Special Issue.

—. "Caste as Language-Weave: Exceeding Sociological Readings of Caste, Span." *Journal of the South Pacific Association of Commonwealth Literature and Language Studies*.52.

—. "The Literature of Dispossession: Subversion of Elitist Nationalism in Dalit and Aboriginal Texts." in Phil Butterrs, Caroline Guerin and Amanda Nettlebeck, Eds. *Crossing Lines: Formations of Australian Culture, Adelaide: Association for the Study of Australian Literature*.

—. "Their History, (Y)our Memories: Provincializing Europe in Dalit Historiography." in Jacqueline Lo et al. Eds. *Impossible Selves: Cultural Readings of Identity*, Melbourne: Australian Scholarly Publishing.

—. "Velutha, Ammu, Death: The Aporia of the Aesthetic." *Words for their own Sake: Literature in The Age of Economic Rationalism*. Eds. Jan Lloyd Jones and Kathie Barnes, Melbourne: Australian Scholarly Publishing.

—. "'English "Gift": The Role of English Bhikkus in Indian Dalit Buddhist Conversions: 1970-1990." *JSL: Journal of the School of Languages and Culture Studies*. JNU, New Delhi, No. 4, Autumn.

Guru, Gopal. "The Interface Between Ambedkar and the Dalit Cultural Movement in Maharastra." in Ghanshyam Shah ed. *Dalit Identity and Politics: Cultural Subordination and the Dalit Challenge*, Vol. 2. New Delhi: Sage Publications, 2001.

Harrison, Selig S. 1956, "Caste and the Andhra Communists." *The American Political Science Review,* Vol. L, No. 2.

Ilaiah, Kancha, "Caste or Class or Caste-Class: A Study in Dalit Bahujan Consciousness in Andhra Pradesh in 1980s." *History and Society: Research in Progress Papers*. New Delhi: NMML, 1995.

Kanungo, Sukla Deb, 1993, "Dalit Women's Search for Identity." *Social Action*, Vol. 43, No. 4.

Kothari, Rita. "Short story in Gujarati Dalit Literature." *Economic and Political Weekly* (Nov, 30, 2001).

Lal, A.C., Bishop. "Foreword." *Dalit Solidarity*, ed. Bhagwan Das and James Massey, xii-xvi. Delhi: ISPCK,1995.

Mosse, D. "Idioms of Subordination and Styles of Protest among Christian and Hindu Harijan Castes in Tamil Nadu." *Contributions to Indian Sociology, n.s.* 28(1), 1994: 67-106.

—. *Baluta*. Bombay: Granthali Publications, 1978.

Paranjape, Makarand. "Caste of Indian English Novel." *Economic and Political Weekly*. (Oct 5, 1991) 2298-2301.

Purushotham, K. "Prosifying Poesy: A Dalit Critique of Modernisation of Telugu." *South India Journal of Social Sciences*. IX: 2 (December 2011): 40-48.Reprinted in *Economic and Political Weekly*. XLIX No 6 (February 8, 2014): 39-43.

—. "Evolution of Telugu Dalit Writing." *Economic and Political Weekly*. ZLV: 22 (May 29, 2010): 55-63.

—. "Gendering Caste: Emergence of Dalit Feminism." *Kakatiya Journal of English Studies*. Vol. 30 (2011): 43-48.

—. "Telangana, Land, Dalits: A Literary Perspective." *The Idea of Telangana*. Ed. G. Akut, Warangal: Akut, 2013: 181-94.

—. "Movement Literature in Telugu: A Dalit Critique." in *Dalit Movements and Literature,* Ed. B. Krishnaiah. New Delhi: Prestige, 2011: 123-37.

—. "Social Justice and Empowerment through English Education." in *Education and Social Empowerment in India,* Ed. Ghanta Chakrapani. New Delhi: Milind Books, 2008: 277-82.

—. "Social Movements and Identity Formation: A Study in Historical Outline." in *Dalit Movements and Literature,* Ed. B. Krishnaiah. New Delhi: Prestige, 2011: 58-66.

—. "Sociology of Literature: Defiance in Telugu Dalit Writings." *Sociologist.* 1: 2 (2007): 406-14.

—. "Telugu Dalit Poetry: An Overview." *Triveni.* 78: 2 (April-June, 2009): 53-56.

—. "The Rise of Telugu Novel: A Dalit Critique." *Kakatiya Journal of English Studies.* Vol. 31 (2012): 64-74.

—. "Two Sari-Ends in Two Telugu Poems: An Anti-Generic Critique of Feminism." *Kakatiya Journal of English Studies.* Vol. 30 (2011): 114-23.

—. "Writing the Self in Telugu Dalit Literature, *Journal of Literature and Aesthetics.* 9: 1 and 2 (Jan-Dec 2009): 277-88.

—. "Centering the Margins: Vemula Yellaiah's *Kakka."* in *Dalits and Social Marginalisation.* Ed. J. Bheemaiah. Jaipur: Avishkar Publishers, 2012: 1-9.

—."Black Masks and Red Writing: A Reading of Kalyana Rao's *Untouchable Spring." Kakatiya Journal of English Studies.* Vol. 27 (2007-08): 63-71.

Patil, Sharad (1988) "Brahmin, Marxist and Dalit: Three Trends in Literature." *Dalit Voice.* 7 (20) (September): 1-15.

Punalekar, S.P. (1988) "Identities and Consciousness: An Overview of Dalit Literature in Maharashtra." *Man and Development,* 10(4) (December).

Ramakrishna V., "Literary and Theater Movements in Colonial Andhra: Struggle for Left Ideological Legitimacy." *Social Scientist,* Vol. 21, Nos 1-2 (1993).

Ramakrishnan, E.V. "Self and Society, The Dalit Subject and the Discourse of Autobiography." *Littcrit 33.* 1 (June 2007): 96-108.

Satyanarayana, A. "Dalit Protest Literature in Telugu: A Historical Perspective." Dalits and Uppercastes: Essays in Social History, New Delhi: Kanishka Publishers, Distributors, 2005.

Satyanarayana, K. "The Discovery of Jashua: The Shaping of Dalit Literary Tradition in Telugu." *Language Forum*, Vol.33: No. 1. Jan-June 2007, 99-11.

—. "Politics of (Self)-Representation: Case of a 'De-Brahminised' Brahmin." *EPW* (Nov 23, 1991).

Srinivas, T. et. al. "Dimensions of Dalit Problems in Post-Independence Period-Socio Literary Movements in Andhra Pradesh." *Kakatiya University Journal of Social Sciences* 1. 2 (Jan-June 2006): 223-31.

Suneetha Rani, K. "Does Translation Empower a Dalit Text?" *Language Forum: a Journal of language and Literature*. Vol. 33: No. 1 (Jan-June 2007).

—. "Dalit Literature for Children" in *Leaves from Your Own Book: Papers in Honour of Sudhakar Marathe*. Ed. Sachidananda Mohanty et al. Delhi: Authors Press, 2009: 133-146.

Swaroopa Rani, Challapalli. "Dalit Women's Writing in Telugu." *Economic and Political Weekly*. April 25, 1998.

Tirumala Rao, Jayadheer, "Hidden Culture of Depressed Castes: A Case Study of Dakkali – A Dalit Community." in Ed. R. Soma Reddy et al. *Castes, Community and Culture in Andhra Desa: 17th and 18th Century,* Hyderabad: Osmania University, 1995.

Alladi Uma and M. Sridhar (Guest Editors). "Dalit Poetry in Telugu." New Delhi:*The Book Review*. Vol XVI,No 2(Feb.2002), 2002.

Yellaiah, Vemula. "Our Exit from the left was the Beginning of the Dalit Writing." interviewed by K. Purushotham and J. Bheemaiah, *Journal of Literature and Aesthetics*. 9: 1&2 (Jan-Dec 2009).

Alladi Uma, Sridhar,M.etal. The Black Rainbow. Hyderabad:Milind Publications, 2002.

SPECIAL ISSUES

Special Issue on "Telugu Dalit Literature." *Indian Literature* 166 (Mar-April 1995).

Special Issue on "Indian Dalit Literature." *Journal of Literature and Aesthetics*, Consultant Editor, K. Purushotham. Vol. 9 No. 1&2 (Jan-Dec 2009).

Muse India Feature: Telugu Dalit Poetry. special editor, Purushotham.K. *http://www.museindia.com/viewarchive.asp?myr=2007&issid=16.* web.

Index